NO MATTER WHAT

THE ART OF GOING FOR IT

By KEVIN KNOX

Unless indicated, all Scripture quotations are taken from The Holy Bible, New International Version®, NIV® Copyright © 1973, 1978, 1984, 2011 by Biblica, Inc.® Used by permission. All rights reserved worldwide.

"Scripture also taken from The Message. Copyright © 1993, 1994, 1995, 1996, 2000, 2001, 2002. Used by permission of NavPress Publishing Group."

Scripture also taken from the Holy Bible, New Living Translation, copyright ©1996, 2004, 2007 by Tyndale House Foundation. Used by permission of Tyndale House Publishers, Inc., Carol Stream, Illinois 60188. All rights reserved.

Formatting by Reddovedesign.com
Funded by Indiegogo: (igg.me/at/nomatterwhat)
Produced by BookRally:

www.bookrally.com

Printed in the United States of America
24 23 22 21 20 19 18 17 16 1 2 3 4 5 6
ISBN-13 (trade paper): 978-1-942306-88-7

Table of Contents

PART FOUR: EXCUSES

PART FIVE: OTHERS

PART SIX: COMMITMENT

On Courage

Whatever courage I have was first given to me by my father.

I remember one night as a kid, confused and unable to sleep, I kept worrying about what I should be when I grew up. Three times, I ran downstairs and asked my dad what he thought. Each time, he did his best to encourage me. On the third trip, he said these words:

"Kevin, you can be whoever you want to be. Whatever you choose, wherever you go- your mother and I will love you.

"No matter what, we'll love you."

As you strive to realize your God-given potential, may you always remember that God loves you like that, with a no-matter-what kind of love.

Author's Note

Wisdom is the ability to know what's right and true. It's a soundness of action, the capacity to live your life with experience, knowledge, and good judgment. *No Matter What* is a book of wisdom. The 100 chapters that follow aim to encourage you to reach out for the person God created you to be, to live your life with knowledge and understanding.

Over the years, I've had hundreds—if not thousands—of conversations with student-athletes and coaches about the struggles they face. *No Matter What* highlights the ten most consistent themes of these discussions. Perhaps the best way to read this book is to read a chapter a day and take time to reflect upon the questions at the end of each. You can begin with part one and read straight through to the end. Or, you can take a section that seems particularly relevant to where you are in this season of life, read through it, and then choose another.

However you go about it, my prayer is that you will be encouraged as you read this book. May you gain courage and wisdom as you go for it, whatever it may be for you.

IDENTITY

PART ONE

The Truest Thing About You

I have loved you with an everlasting love.
Jeremiah 31:3

Life is not a matter of creating a special name for ourselves,
but of uncovering the name we have always had.
Richard Rohr

ONE OF THE greatest lies in the world today is that you only matter if you prove yourself an exception to the rest.

Win.
Set records.
Do something no one's ever done.

But, what if life's not about proving yourself? What if who you are isn't attached to what you do?

If you're like me, the drive to be exceptional—to stand out from the crowd—is innate. There's a constant pressure to keep up with those around me, to keep up appearances, to keep outdoing myself and to impress people.

It's exhausting.

Without thinking, I work really hard to make sure everyone knows just how great I am. We all do this. However subtly, we over-name, over-validate, and over-congratulate ourselves at nearly every turn. The prophet Jeremiah has hopeful words for us, though. Jeremiah says, "God loves you with an everlasting love."

Everlasting. That word means eternal. It means endless, undying, enduring, infinite, and boundless. If what Jeremiah says is true, then long before you did anything to stand out, before you won a scholarship or went undefeated or earned the praise of your peers, God's love was there for you.

You were enough.
Before you did anything.
You were enough.

And long after you've set your records and made your name known, years from now when the trophies are covered in dust and no one knows who you are, God's love will be as strong for you then as it is today.

So, who are you, really?

Are you an accomplished athlete or coach? Are you your best day? Do your successes or failures define you? According to Jeremiah, who you are at your core—your truest self—has nothing to do with any of that. You are a child of God, loved wholly and completely. This is the truest thing about you. This truth isn't something you earn; it's something you receive. In fact, this everlasting love is something you received long ago, before you ever proved anything to anybody.

Your true self is such good news. Your true self is everlasting. It is endless, undying, enduring, infinite, and boundless. Your true self cannot be offended. It is not tied to victories or wealth or fame or anything else.

Yes, there are other truths. You have gifts. You have talent. There is perhaps a drive within you to do something meaningful with those gifts and talents. These truths are important too, and we'll spend a great deal of time in the pages that follow talking about how to do just that. It's just that some truths aren't the truest thing about you. The fact that God loves you, that's the truest thing.

So, who are you, really?
What's the truest thing about you?
What things in your life compete with the truest thing?

No Matter What...

God loves you with an everlasting love. That's the truest thing about you. Live from that love today.

Why God Loves You

And so we know and rely on the love God has for us. God is love.
Whoever lives in love lives in God, and God in them.
1 John 4:16

Behold the one beholding you and smiling.
Anthony De Mello

WHY DOES GOD love you?

A couple of years ago, there was a running back (I'll call him Tony) whose world briefly fell apart. In four years at Cal, Tony rarely played. Just before his senior season, Tony began to show some promise. He worked his way up the depth chart, and there was a good chance he'd be a starter his final year on campus. Unfortunately for Tony, though, he injured his hip only two weeks before fall camp. Devastated, his injury forced him to miss all of camp and much of the following season. He never started a game and only played sparingly when he did see the field.

As is the case for a lot of guys, football was everything for Tony. In high school, he was first team all-state; his team won a couple of state championships, and Tony was heavily recruited.

When he came to Cal, much of his identity and all of his confidence came from the fact that he was a good football player. To make matters worse, Tony's dad, who'd been absent for most of Tony's childhood, finally began to show interest in his son only after Tony started making headlines because of football. The idea that football wouldn't be a part of his life anymore completely floored Tony. Who was Tony now? Why would anyone care about him? What about his dad? Would he still want to be a part of Tony's life?

Which brings me back to my first question: Why do you think God loves you?

Does God love you because of a talent or an ability you possess?
Does God love you because of how successful you are at using that talent or ability?
Does God love you because of anything you do or don't do?

These are big questions, important questions. The task of nearly all the world's religions is to answer these questions. These questions are why I have a job as a pastor, and they're why a book like this is even necessary. Knowing why God loves you is one of the most important things you can know.

So, why does God love you? First John 4:16, after inviting us to "know and rely on the love God has for us," says this, "God is love."

That's the answer.
God is love.

Every talented, successful, and driven person on the planet needs to hear this.
God is love.

The starting place for understanding why God loves you, why God loves anybody, is understanding that God is love. At the core of God's being, the very essence of God's character, is love. Before God is anything, God is love. The Scriptures say God is creator. Well, before God created anything, God was love. All God's creativity stems from God's love. They say God is a provider. Again, all God's provision comes first from God's generous heart of love. Some passages say God is a refuge. If that's the case, it's only because God is first a loving God who desires to protect those in need.

So, why does God love you?

The truth is, God doesn't love you because of anything you've done. God doesn't love you because of your talent, your good deeds, or even your beliefs. God doesn't love you because of anything you did or didn't do. God loves you because of who God is.

Do you believe God loves you no matter what?
Is it hard for you to accept this love? Why?
What would it take for you to "know and rely on" God's love today?

No Matter What...

The no matter what-ness of God's love is vast and beyond measure. God loves you not because of who you are or what you've done; God loves you because of who God is, period.

Quit Proving Yourself

When God approves of your life, even your
enemies will end up shaking your hand.
Proverbs 16:7 (MSG)

I don't have to show anything to anyone.
There is nothing to prove.
Cristiano Ronaldo

WHAT DO YOU have to prove?

Ours is a culture of bigger, faster, stronger. We celebrate the youngest to accomplishment, the quickest to the top, and the richest among us. I call it "prove-yourself" economics.

In sports, prove-yourself economics is everything. When competing at the highest levels, being bigger, faster, or stronger goes a long way. But as athletes at the highest level, it's important to remember God's economy is altogether different.

God's economy is not a prove-yourself economy.

In prove-yourself economics, you have to constantly fight for the acceptance of others. In God's economy, you're accepted from day one. In prove-yourself economics, success and failure define who you are. In God's economy, what God thinks of you defines who you are. In prove-yourself economics, you're only as good as your last play. In God's economy, the next play is the most important.

In prove-yourself economics, fear drives us forward. In God's economy, perfect love drives out fear.

Maybe the most concise way to say it: In prove-yourself economics, you have to fight for love. In God's economy, you're loved already. In fact, that might be the best way to describe the gospel:

We live from God's love, not for it.

A friend of mine, Aaron Loy, says, "You are not your reputation. You are not your past. You are not what you did. You are who God says you are."

Proverbs 16:7 says that when God approves of your life, even your enemies take notice. And herein lies the good news: God does approve of your life. He loves you wholly and completely, today, just as you are. That's the truest thing about you.

Now, of course the desire to prove yourself can be a strong motivator. I'm sure many underdog athletes who defied the odds and achieved something great utilized the prove-yourself mindset to their advantage. I just don't believe it's the best way to live.

Playing a sport, perfecting a craft, or living your life in order to prove yourself is still just, in the end, a life lived for the approval of others.

God's love is never attached to wins and losses, success or failure. His love for you cannot be offended and it will not go away. You don't have to prove yourself with God.

Where do feel like you have to prove yourself?
Why do you feel this way?

Reread Proverbs 16:7. Ask God to make you more aware of His love and approval in your life.

No Matter What...

You don't have to prove anything to anybody. God loves you already. Now, today. Start here, then from this healthy place, go realize your athletic, artistic, and creative potential.

Your True Self

Though your riches increase,
Do not set your heart on them.
Psalm 62:10

The man who views the world at fifty
the same as he did at twenty has wasted
thirty years of his life.
Mohammad Ali

THE PROBLEM WITH living your life focused on proving yourself is that the debt is never paid.

The work is never done.
Your ego is never satisfied.
There's always someone better.

A few years ago, there was a superstar athlete at Cal who was having quite a season. He was one of the best players in the conference, if not the country, at his position, and speculation was growing that if he decided to forgo his senior season, he'd be a top NFL draft pick later that spring. He and I sat down together just before the season was over. We talked about the decision before him, and I asked him how he was dealing with all the pressure. His answer to me was nothing short of perfect. "I'm doing alright," he said, "because I'm more than a football player. What happens on the field doesn't define me."

I was taken aback. He was saying to me the very thing I'd hoped to share with him. It was the reason I'd asked him to coffee in the first place. He went on, "I attended this football camp in high school, and there was this guy there. He was a former NFL great at my position. He gave us a speech saying, 'Never define yourself by the position you play in football. This game comes and goes. Who you are is much bigger.'"

Who you are is much bigger.

Psalm 62:10 says, "Though your riches increase, do not set your heart on them." In other words, stay grounded. Know the difference between who you are and the sport you play.

Life is largely a matter of letting go of your ego. If you define yourself by talent or intelligence or position, then whenever someone doesn't recognize these things, you're offended. But what part of you is offended? It's always your ego, never your true self in God. When you get offended, it's always the position you play that's offended, never the person you truly are.

You are more than an athlete.
You are more than a position.
You are more than a student or a coach or an artist.
Talent, wealth, and fame do not define you.

You are a child of God, loved wholly and completely; this is what defines you.

May today be the day you no longer have to build, protect, or promote yourself. May the work that you do be about steward-ship and service, not ego. May the weight of the world lift from your shoulders, and may you discover the peace you've been looking for. That peace has nothing to do with accomplish-ment or position or what role you play in the world.

What are some of the differences between the sport you play and the person you truly are?

What would it look like for you to give up the need to prove yourself, and at the same time, continue to pursue your God-given potential with everything you've got?

No Matter What...

God loves you. That never changes. That's the truest thing about you. Realizing your God-given potential isn't about proving yourself to God. It's about knowing you have nothing to prove, and from that healthy place, using your gifts and talents to bless the world around you.

From Striving to Abiding

Abide in me, as I also abide in you. No branch
can bear fruit by itself; it must remain in the vine.
Neither can you bear fruit unless you remain in me.
John 15:4

Keep your dreams alive. Understand to achieve
anything requires faith and belief in yourself,
vision, hard work, determination, and dedication.
Remember, all things are possible for
those who believe.
Gail Devers

Strive *(verb):* (1) make great efforts to achieve or obtain
something. (2) struggle or fight vigorously.

Abide *(verb):* (1) accept or act in accordance with (2) adhere to,
stick to, or stand beside.

WHETHER YOU'RE AN athlete or a coach, an artist or a
creative, it's important to remember the tension between striving and abiding.

To realize your full creative potential, striving is required. Nothing just happens. You have to reach out to achieve anything. At
the same time, striving doesn't define you. If you achieve suc-

cess or realize a goal, the reality of who you are hasn't shifted. At the end of the day, you're just as loved by God as you were when the day you began. Win or lose. Succeed or fail. God invites us all to both strive toward achievement and abide in His love. So how does one live in the tension between striving and abiding?

A few suggestions:

When you compete, don't compare.
Give each day your all, and when go to bed at night, know that who you are at your core hasn't changed. If the results weren't what you wanted, don't envy your opponent. Rest in what God thinks of you, and wake up the next day determined to further perfect your craft. Remember, God never looked in your mirror and wished He saw someone else. Compete, but don't compare.

When you win, celebrate, but don't gloat.
Nobody likes a sore loser, and everyone disdains an arrogant winner. Be gracious when you win. Receive it as a gift. Winning is a blessing; no one's entitled to it. Knute Rockne said, "One man practicing sportsmanship is far better than 50 preaching it." When you win, celebrate, but don't gloat.

When you lose, learn from it.
Failure is a great teacher. When you lose, congratulate your opponent, examine what went wrong, and learn from it. Don't wallow in defeat. Accept it, adjust, and move on.

When unfriendly critics speak out, ignore them.
Cynicism often passes for insight, but don't be fooled. There's always somebody saying you can't do it, and those people have to be ignored. Know the difference between a friendly critic

and an unfriendly one. The former is trying to help you. The latter only wants to see you fall.

Begin every day by abiding in God's love.
Whatever it means for you, seek God each day. For some, this means beginning the day with prayer. For others, it means reading the Bible or a book like this. It could mean getting together with a friend for encouragement or taking a walk to clear your head. Whatever it takes for you to remind yourself that God loves you, go to that space daily. Regardless of what happens on the field of play, remember your true self in God. After you abide in God's love, go work on your craft. Use it to bless everyone around you.

Where are you striving?
How are you abiding?
Which is defining you more these days?

No Matter What...

Striving and abiding are two things you have to embrace at the same time. Strive to serve. Serve to grow. Abide in God's love the whole way.

There's No "There" There

Those who find me find life and
receive favor from the Lord.
Proverbs 8:35

Number one is just to gain a passion for running.
To love the morning, to love the trail, to love the
pace on the track. And if some kid gets really
good at it, that's cool, too.
Pat Tyson

"THERE'S NO THERE there. Enjoy the journey."

I first heard these words when I was 17. The real-life Rudy, from the movie *Rudy*, came to my high school and spoke to us about dreams. He talked about accomplishing goals in life and enjoying the journey along the way.

Rudy, if you don't know the story, was an undersized, walk-on defensive lineman at the University of Notre Dame in the 1970s. After much adversity and awe-inspiring determination, Rudy dressed for the final game of his collegiate career. He played the game's last two plays, sacking the opposing team's quarterback as time expired. He was carried off the field as the crowd chanted his name, a feat the movie says hasn't happened since.

Rudy told us, though, that after accomplishing what he accomplished at Notre Dame and later in Hollywood, he felt unsatisfied. At Notre Dame, he'd told himself, "Once I get to play, I'll have arrived. I'll have made it as a human being." But when he reached that goal, he said it wasn't enough. So, he set another goal.

"Once I tell my story and make this movie, I'll have arrived." But again, realizing that goal left him wanting. Then he realized, "After years of setting goals and getting there, I learned there's no there there. I decided life is about the journey. It's about me growing as an individual along the way."

What do you think?

If you could just get there, would your life finally mean something? Where is there? What does it look like?
How will your core identity be any different there than it is here, now?

If you're unable to find happiness here, I promise you won't find it there. It's possible to spend all your time focused on where you'll end up someday, all the while forgetting that today is a place you once longed to be. Stop pursuing happiness. Realize that happiness is in the pursuit. I believe everything you need to be satisfied, to experience joy, and to sense the presence of God is available to you today, in this place.

Somewhere else doing something else is no way to live.

God is not waiting on the other side of some accomplishment or the realization of a dream.

God is present here and now, today, in this moment.

No Matter What...

There's no there there. Enjoy the journey. This season. These players. This workout. Today.

Who You Become > Where You End Up

Better a patient person than a warrior, one with
self-control than one who takes a city.
Proverbs 16:32

Sports creates a bond between contemporaries that
lasts a lifetime. It also gives your life structure, discipline
and a genuine, sincere, pure fulfillment that few
other areas of endeavor provide.
Bob Cousy

WHO ARE YOU becoming?

A goal of mine this year is to run 400 miles. Yes, that's a big
number. But, if I average 8 miles per week, I'll get there by the
end of December. As I write this, I'm 150.33 miles in, 38 percent of the way there and on track to reach my goal.

However, today—150 miles in—my perspective on 400 miles
has changed a bit.

If and when I finally reach my goal, this journey will represent so much more than merely logging 400 miles. Already, it

represents a dozen or so runs in January and February with a friend recovering from an ankle injury. It represents another 20 runs I absolutely didn't want to take, either because of the weather or just because I didn't feel like it; I ran anyway and am better for it.

It includes at least two half-marathons, one where I didn't feel so well, but gave it my all and got a new personal record. It represents the run I took earlier this week. I planned on running three miles, but took a wrong turn and ended up running seven—a lesson in frustration, perseverance, and just finishing what I started.

Four hundred will include windy runs, runs in the rain, hot runs, hilly runs, being chased by a dog for ¼ mile in late April, and at least 1,000 waves to fellow runners I saw along the way. Prayers. Thoughts. Sights. Sounds. Sweat. Aches. And a handful of close calls with cars pulling out in front of me.

The best part of 400 miles won't be getting there. The best part of 400 miles will be who I became along the way.

Whether you're an athlete, an artist, or just somebody with an idea trying to give something to the world, getting there won't be nearly as valuable as all the things you'll learn along the way. God's gift to you won't be the finish line; it'll be the person you became while running the race.

How are you different today than the day this all began?
How is God using your circumstances to shape you?
Where do you need to be more patient with God, to loosen your grip on where this is all headed and simply allow God to work with you today?

No Matter What...

Enjoy the run today. Take it in. If you fall, get back up. If you make a wrong turn, keep running. Who you become is always more important than where you end up.

It's Not About You

> Start with God—the first step in learning is
> bowing down to God; only fools thumb their
> noses at such wisdom and learning.
> Proverbs 1:7 (MSG)

> I'm a part of a team, and I'm no better or any worse
> than any single player on this team. That's the approach
> I've always had and will continue to have. It's not about me.
> It's never been all about me. If it had, this would have
> been a really lonely journey.
> Mia Hamm

NONE OF THIS is only about you.

Today, you didn't wake up into a movie called *Your Life* starring you. Your friends and family aren't supporting characters. The people you pass on the streets and don't know, they're not extras.

This place isn't only about your glory, your advancement, or you realizing your dreams.

The sooner you embrace this fact, the sooner you'll find the freedom God wants for you.

Serving in the role that I do, I meet a lot of guys who think their sport is only all about them, especially when they first arrive on campus. They think, "I'm God's gift to this place." Not just players, but coaches and support staff think this way, too. Shoot, when I first got here, I thought the same way.

This mindset is easy to spot. It's self-centered. It's obsessed with validation. It's often resistant to hardship or struggle. Sometimes, it's unwilling to be coached. It sounds like:

> *"This is going to be easy."*
> *"Injuries only happen to other people."*
> *"If things don't go my way, it's probably someone else's fault."*

Hidden behind each of these statements is much fear and little understanding of our true selves in God.

There was an athlete a few years ago, all-everything in high school, who got injured his first semester on campus. His career continued down that path for a couple of years, often injured, rarely on the field. We sat down together two weeks into his second injury. It took me about thirty seconds to hear it in his language, "Man, if I could just get on the field, we'd be winning…"

"You really think it's that easy?" I asked him. "I don't want to offend you. I'm sure if you were able to play, you'd help the team. But hear me when I say this: you are not God's gift to Cal Football. It's more likely that Cal Football is God's gift to you."

Regardless of who you are or what role you play on the team, yes, God is open to you contributing, perhaps considerably. But, at the end of the day, God cares more about who you're becoming than where you end up. God wants to use this whole journey—the struggle, the work, the successes, and the failures—to shape you into a more whole human being. More than that, God probably wants to use you to shape the people around you.

The opportunities God gives us are rarely only about us.

God's desire for all of us is twofold: (1) God hopes we learn to trust God no matter what, and (2) God invites us to use our gifts and talents to bless other people along the way.

In your heart, is this whole deal only about you?
How can you make it more about other people today?
How is God using this experience to shape you?
How is it God's gift to you?

No Matter What...

Stop making this all about you. Start with God; then, see the people around you. Be a team player, and make it about other people today.

God Doesn't Bless Us with Success

Commit your work to the Lord,
and your plans will be established.
Proverbs 16:3

Treat a person as he is, and he will remain as he is.
Treat him as he could be, and he will become what he should be.
Jimmy Johnson

GOD DOESN'T BLESS us with success. God blesses us with potential.

My first big speaking opportunity came when I was a senior in high school. Up to that point, I hadn't spoken much in public. But the little I had apparently caught the eye of somebody, because at eighteen years old, I was invited to speak at all three services of my parents' 2,000+ member church.

At the time, I really didn't know what I was doing. I knew what I liked to listen to, though, so I decided to imitate that. I scribbled down a few notes, included a funny story or two, and I chose to have only one main point. For all intents and purposes, I hit it out of the park.

Standing at the door as people exited the church services, I was greeted with hundreds of folks saying things like, "Wow. Great message!" and "God's got big things in store for you some day." And "Thank you. God used you today."

For the seventeen-year-old version of myself, it was all a bit much. I knew I enjoyed being in front of people, but I'd never considered I had an actual God-given gift for public speaking.

Just before I went to bed that night, I got down on my knees and acknowledged to God that God had blessed me, not necessarily with a great talk or even the praise from all those people. Really, outside of that morning, I hadn't experienced a whole lot of success with my speaking abilities at all. No, that night, I simply prayed, thanking God for my gift. It occurred to me that God had blessed me, not with success, but with potential and an opportunity to use it. Somehow, I knew if I stewarded it well, I could keep using it to serve a lot of people.

Here's my point: your talent, your God-given ability of athleticism or speed or size or coordination, or all of the above, is God's blessing to you. God's blessing isn't you winning a championship with that talent or becoming rich and famous because of that talent. God's blessing is the talent; it's the opportunity before you.

Regardless of how you define success, God's already blessed you. Even before you succeed or fail in using your gift or talent, the blessing is present. What you do with this blessing is, in large part, not up to God; it's up to you.

What gifts or talents has God blessed you with?
What potential has He placed inside of you?

Talent and opportunity are God's blessings to you. Success is a choice you make yourself. Whether it's speaking in public, blocking a linebacker, or calling plays, God's blessed you already.

No Matter What...

God doesn't bless you with a win or curse you with a loss. God blesses you with potential. Success is a choice you make, not God.

Talent Is Never Enough

Those who trust in their riches will fall,
but the righteous will thrive like a green leaf.
Proverbs 11:28

Gold medals aren't really made of gold.
They're made of sweat, determination, and a hard-to-find alloy
called guts.
Dan Gable

WHAT'S MORE VALUABLE: talent or character?

I'm convinced the people with the most talent in the world mostly go unnoticed. We only know the ones who work hard and persevere.

Ask any 5-star prospect who never cracked the starting lineup. Ask every 2-star athlete who became an all-American. Realizing God-given potential has less to do with innate talent and more to do with your character. Things like work ethic, the ability to overcome obstacles, a commitment to get better every day—no matter what—these are the characteristics of someone who realizes his or her creative potential.

There was a study done of the two 2015 NFL Super Bowl teams. It found that the average "star-rating" of each roster coming out of high school was just 2.4 stars. On a scale of 2 to 5 stars, that's just above the lowest rating possible. Translation: talent doesn't prove anything. Sure, it might get you in the room, but it's not an accurate indicator of future success. Sports, like all of life, are about substance, not form.

The fact that character is more important than talent is good news for all of us. Talent is innate, meaning it's fixed. You can't change the level of the talent God gave you. But character? Character is something you can always change. Habits, work ethic, integrity: these things you control.

Here are ten character traits that require absolutely no talent to possess:

Attitude
Energy
Effort
Work ethic
Body language
Coachability
Preparedness
Perseverance
Positivity
Being a team player

The shape of your future isn't about what some recruiter says you're worth. The true shape of your future is your character. It's the sum total of the choices you'll make today and the effort you're willing to put forth tomorrow.

Are you relying only on your talent?
How hard are you willing to work toward realizing what's in front of you?
What aspects of your character do you need to work on today?

No Matter What...

Talent is never enough. To perfect your craft: commit, improve a little each day, and be willing to persevere when things get tough.

PURPOSE

PART TWO

Know Why

Where there is no vision, the people perish.
Proverbs 29:18

Burnout is more often caused by a purpose
deficiency than a vitamin deficiency.
Remember your why.
Jon Gordon

WHY ARE YOU doing this?

When my wife and I found out she was pregnant with our first son, Zander, I made a decision: leading a healthy lifestyle was no longer optional. It had to be done. So what did I do? I ate better, I started running, and in the nine months that followed, I lost 20 pounds.

For years, I'd wanted to take better care of myself physically but hadn't. I tried all sorts of diets and cleanses; nothing stuck. I'd often imagine the life I could live or the life I should live, thinking, *One day, I'll get back into shape.* But burnout after burnout left me thinking, *Maybe I'm just not trying hard enough* or *Perhaps I'll never get back into shape.*

But when Zander was born, everything changed.
What changed exactly?

My *why*.

The arrival of Zander shifted my life's priorities. I decided the best gift I could give my new son was a healthy dad. I decided professionally, spiritually, and physically, I would be at the top of my game when he joined our family. After years of wandering in the desert from diet to cleanse, from exercise fad to new mountain bike—once my why became clear, I finally got committed.

Your why is your vision. It's what you're really after in life. It's not something that changes with the shifting winds. It's a commitment. Knowing why with clarity is extremely important. If your why is foggy, you won't be committed when things get tough. Here are three signs your why isn't clear enough:

You try all the time.
Trying is something uncommitted people do. When you have a clear vision, when you know what you're after, you either do it or you don't. There is no middle ground of trying.

You talk about what could happen.
When you don't know your why, you live in a world of could and should. With a clear why, though, what must happen is the only thing that matters. What could happen and what should happen aren't things you think about because you're too busy being committed to what must happen.

You complain a lot.
In my view, complaints are a by-product of a foggy vision. When you're commitments are unclear, circumstances rule the

day. You don't see where you're going, so you end up complaining about the struggles you are facing. Reread the last 3 sentences. Every time you complain, it's a sign your vision isn't clear enough. If you complained today, your why isn't clear enough.

Clarify your why. Commit to it. Stop daydreaming about what could or what should happen. Know your why, and follow through.

What's your why? What are you after?
Is could or should a part of your vocabulary? What must happen today?
What do you complain about? How can a clearer vision help you stop complaining?

No Matter What...

Know your why. Get clear on where you're going and what must happen for you to get there.

Set Goals

Wise people think before they act;
Fools don't—and even brag about their foolishness.
Proverbs 13:16 (NLT)

If you don't know where you're going,
you'll end up somewhere else.
Yogi Berra

WHAT GOALS DO you have for yourself?

A study of the 1979 Harvard MBA program proves that it pays to set goals. That year, students were asked, "Have you set clear, written goals for your future and made plans to accomplish them?"

The results of the study are staggering.

3 percent of respondents said they both set goals and wrote them down. 13 percent said they set goals but failed to write them down. The remaining 84 percent responded they neither set goals, nor wrote anything down.

Fast-forward 10 years.

The 13 percent who said they set goals but didn't write them down earned twice as much as the 84 percent who set no goals. The remaining 3 percent, who both set goals and wrote them down, earned 10 times more than the other 97 percent combined annually.[1]

Literally, it pays to set goals and write them down.

Proverbs 13:16 says, "Wise people think before they act." Wisdom isn't about what you know or don't know. Wisdom is about what you do. Think before you act, then act. A key step in you realizing your God-given potential is as simple as pulling out a piece of paper and writing down some goals for yourself. Not much else needs to be said.

Know your why. Set goals. Write them down.

No Matter What...

It pays to set goals and write them down. The difference between a daydream and reality is you writing down where it is you want to go.

Make a Plan

In their hearts humans plan their course,
but the Lord establishes their steps.
Proverbs 16:9

A goal without a plan is just a wish.
Antoine de Saint-Exupéry

WHAT'S YOUR PLAN?

I've started at least five major writing projects in the last two years that sit unfinished. Yes, I had a vision for what I wanted to write. I even set goals for each of the projects and wrote them down. But the one thing I failed to do was to make a plan for their completion.

Whether it's writing a book, selling a piece of art, or winning the Rose Bowl, you won't get very far without a plan. Unfortunately, most of us spend more time planning our two-week summer vacation than we do planning the other 50 weeks of the year.

Your plan doesn't have to be fancy.
It just needs to exist.

To realize my goal of running 400 miles this year, I made a plan to run 8 miles a week. What that means for me is this: every week I run two 3-mile runs and one 2-mile run. I run once on Monday, again on Wednesday, and my final run of the week is on Friday or Saturday. One of the reasons creating a plan works is because I don't waste additional mental energy or stress thinking about how I'm going to reach my goal.

There's a phenomenon in psychology called the Zeigarnik Effect. It describes the mind's tendency to worry about projects we start but haven't completed. The worry the Zeigarnik Effect describes isn't about the project itself, the creativity or the problem solving required within the project; no, it describes worry surrounding the completion of the project, whether or not we'll have enough time to finish the work and if our efforts will be enough to actually find a solution. By definition, the Zeigarnik Effect frustrates our ability to actually execute the project. Our creative energy is depleted because we're worried about finishing the work instead of using our minds to create new solutions.

Establishing a plan, though, fights against the Zeigarnik Effect. It reduces the stress surrounding the project in front of you. You don't have to worry about how something is going to get done; you just have to work the plan.

Where are you going?
Do you know your why?
Have you set clear, measurable goals and written them down?

Great, now make a plan. Once you do, you'll be free to focus on today.

No Matter What...

Goals mean very little without a plan. Know why. Set goals. Make a plan and commit to it.

Measure Your Days

Teach us to number our days,
that we may gain a heart of wisdom.
Psalm 90:12

You find that you have peace of mind when you
know that it was a 100% effort that you gave, win or lose.
Gordie Howe

WHAT WOULD IT take for you to make the most of today?

In her book, *The Top Five Regrets of the Dying*, nurse Bronnie Ware says the number one regret of palliative care patients just before they died is "I wish I'd had the courage to live a life true to myself." Ware writes:

> "This was the most common regret of all. When people realise that their life is almost over and look back clearly on it, it is easy to see how many dreams have gone unfulfilled. Most people had not honoured even a half of their dreams and had to die knowing that it was due to choices they had made, or not made. Health brings a freedom very few realise, until they no longer have it."[2]

At the end of your life, you won't regret all the television you didn't watch. You won't wish that you'd spent more time playing video games or ignoring the people around you. You'll think of this moment and what you did with it.

Let me put it another way: at some point, every athlete retires. Our bodies wear out. Seasons end. And we move on to the next thing. When that time comes, will you think, *I wish I'd had the courage to live a life true to myself?* Will you wish you'd done something different with this season, now?

In Psalm 90:12, the psalmist asks for guidance, saying, "Teach me to number my days, so that I can gain a heart of wisdom." Notice what the psalmist doesn't ask for. The psalmist doesn't say, "Teach me to number my years" or "Teach me to number my seasons." No, the psalmist's request is to know what to do with today.

After you've figured out your why, set your goals, and made your plans, decide what must happen today. Because how you live today is how you'll live every day.

> *What does today offer you that tomorrow won't?*
> *Break down your goals and your plan; what must happen today?*
> *What do you have to be grateful for today?*

Lord, teach us to measure our days, that we may gain a heart of wisdom.

No Matter What...

Today is a gift. There never has been and never will be another day quite like today. Steward it well.

Start

Do not despise the day of small beginnings,
for the LORD rejoices to see the work begin.
Zechariah 4:10

It's the job that's never started that
takes the longest to finish.
JRR Tolkien

GET STARTED.

In the master bathroom of my house, there's a towel rack that hangs on the wall across from the shower. When you open the shower door, it's right there where you need it to be. Unfortunately, about 7 months ago, someone yanked on it, pulling it halfway out of wall. It still worked, but it looked awful and needed fixing for the longest time.

I know this sounds silly, but fixing that towel rack took me 182 days and 10 minutes to complete. That's right. It took me 182 days to start and 10 minutes to screw the rack back into place.

One hundred percent of the things you never start won't get done. James J. Hill said it this way: "You can't build a reputation on what you're going to do."[3] Whether it's fixing a towel rack, writing a letter to a friend, or pursuing a new career: if you never start, you'll never finish.

What do you need to start today?

You know, it's funny. When I share with people that I work with athletes, they often tell me of their athletic accolades. They say things like, "I could've played division 1 football if I wanted" or "I used to be a pretty good this or that. I bet I could've made a short career of it if I'd tried." I usually smile and nod my head.

Unfortunately, my next thought is something I'm not proud of: *Yeah, but you didn't.*

I'm not trying to be judge-y, just honest. It's easy to hide behind what you could have done. That's especially true if you never gave it a shot. By never trying, you never put yourself on the line. And without actually risking failure, you never had to test the reality of what you could or couldn't have accomplished?

It reminds me of sports commentators who critique athletes and coaches over the smallest missteps. Or political pundits who suggest they could do a better job than our current political leaders. If these people could really do better, then why not get in the game?

Quit complaining.
Quit critiquing.
Go for it.
Start.

You'll never achieve the things you said you could've achieved if you never have the guts to start.

What haven't you started that needs to begin today?
What are you waiting for?
Why be afraid?

No Matter What...

The first step, however small, could be the most important step of your life. Go. Start. God celebrates even the smallest of beginnings because the work has finally begun.

Only Do It

Let your eyes look directly forward,
and your gaze be straight before you.
Proverbs 4:25

Self-discipline is the ability to do the
important thing rather than the urgent thing.
Unknown

WHAT DO YOU need to focus on today?

In August 1988, Nike launched one of its most famous ad campaigns. The first commercial of the campaign opened with 80-year-old Walt Stack running across the Golden Gate Bridge. Shirt off, Nike shoes laced up, Walt looked at the camera while running and said, "I run 17 miles every morning. People ask me how I keep my teeth from chattering in the wintertime. That's easy, I leave them in my locker." Panning out, the screen goes black, and for the first time, Nike introduced to the world these three iconic words:

Just do it.

My guess is, you've said these words to yourself at one point or another.

"Just do it, Kevin. Pick up the phone, and make the call."
"Just do it; jump. The water's not that far away."
"Just do it; go win the game."

The problem is, of course, it's usually never that simple. If it was as easy as just do it, you'd have done it already. Saying "just do it" leads me to believe that doing it is only a matter of willpower. There are plenty of things I've wanted to do, even had the willpower to accomplish, but they were never realized.

Writer Phillip Eby talks about the secret meaning of just do it, saying,

> "The trick is in the meaning of the word 'just'. When somebody says, 'just do it', they are trying to communicate that you should not do anything else. It might better be phrased as, 'Only do it, without thinking about anything, not even about what you're doing. In fact, don't even do it, just watch yourself doing it, but don't actually try to do anything.' In other words, the real trick is to stop trying, and start actually doing."[4]

Only do it.

Only do the thing that needs to be done. Think about nothing else. See nothing else. Only do this thing. Now that's helpful.

Our brains weren't designed for multitasking. Psychologists have concluded that multitasking is actually a myth; it's impossible. Neurological studies show that when we attempt to multitask, our brains aren't actually doing two things at once; we're just switching between two or three tasks quickly. They've concluded, what we call multitasking is us attempting multiple actions with deficient skill and competency. We'd be better off just focusing on one thing at a time.

What requires more of your focused attention today?

Are you struggling in a relationship? Spend more time with that person. Do nothing else. Listen. Talk. Communicate. Serve.

Is there a technique related to your craft that isn't sharp enough? Practice. Do nothing else. Work on the technique until you can do it blindfolded.

Multitasking is not your friend. The more focused you are, the more work you get done. Fix your gaze only upon the thing in front of you, and only do it.

No Matter What...

When you only do something, it gets done. Focus. Pay attention to nothing else. Only do it.

Just Get Better

A hard worker has plenty of food,
but a person who chases fantasies
ends up in poverty.
Proverbs 28:19

Don't try to be better than the other guy.
Just try to be better than you were the day
before. That's all you have to do.
Sam Wyche

HOW WILL YOU improve today?

In 1988, Kansas State University's football program was widely considered the worst in the history of the sport. The Wildcats didn't win a single game in 1987 or 1988. They'd never been to a bowl game. With a total of 8 winless seasons, K-State hadn't beaten a ranked team 63 consecutive attempts, and no head coach had exited the school with a winning record.

Then, in 1989, K-State hired Bill Snyder. A man of few words, Coach Snyder's opening press conference offered just one sound bite: "Our goal is to get better every day." And get better they did.

Sports columnist Joe Posnanski highlights Snyder's success, writing,

> "In his first year, Kansas State won one game. Improvement. The Wildcats had a winning record in his third year—just their second winning season in more than 20 years. Kansas State won its first ever bowl game in his fifth year. Kansas State was ranked in the Top 10 two years after that (first time), played on New Year's Day a year after that (first time), and was a fumble away from the national championship game two years after that (obviously, first time). Improvement. All the time."[5]

At this writing, Bill Snyder's record with the Wildcats is 187-94-1. The university named its football stadium after him. The State of Kansas named a highway after him. By nearly every standard, he is among the greatest head coaches of all time.

All he did was get better every day.

Most of us are too shortsighted to imitate the mindset of Bill Snyder. We want tomorrow what only five years of work can produce. We overestimate where we'll be in one year and underestimate where we could be in ten.

How will you get better today?
What's one thing you can improve?

Today, just get better. Improve.

No Matter What...

Focus on improvement. Think long. See ten years ahead, but get better one day at a time.

Just Keep Moving

Give careful thought to the paths for your feet,
and be steadfast in all your ways.
Proverbs 4:26

Continuous effort, not strength or intelligence,
is the key to unlocking our potential.
Liane Cardes

ARE YOU SOMEONE who quits or someone who perseveres?

A young comic once asked Jerry Seinfeld for advice. Seinfeld offered this: "The only way to become a better comic is to write better jokes, and the only way to write better jokes is to write every day."

Seinfeld said when he first started out in comedy, he bought a calendar large enough to show every day of the year on one page, and he hung it in his apartment. He also bought a big red marker. And then, for every day he wrote a new joke, he'd place a red X on the calendar over that day. Seinfeld said, "After a few days, you'll have a chain. Just keep at it and the chain will grow longer every day. You'll like seeing that chain, especially when you get a few weeks under your belt. Your only job is to not break the chain."

Don't break the chain.

Proverbs 4:26 says, "Be steadfast in all your ways." That means today, whatever your craft, work at it. Even if it's just a little, do the work. Do that again tomorrow, and once you get a few days in a row, don't break the chain. Remaining steadfast means you keep pursuing your goal, you keep trusting God, no matter what.

Every football player knows the best way to break a tackle is to keep your feet moving. Walt Disney said it this way: "The difference in winning and losing is most often not quitting." Do the little things today, and then do them again tomorrow and the day after that. And the day after that, and the day after that one. You don't need to arrive tomorrow; all you need is to keep your feet moving today.

What little thing can you do today, repeat tomorrow, and keep going long enough to create a chain?

No Matter What...

Don't break the chain. Remain steadfast in all you do. Just keep moving.

You Don't Have a Life; You Have a Day

The soul of the sluggard craves and gets
nothing, while the soul of the diligent
is richly supplied.
Proverbs 13:4

Success isn't owned. It's leased,
and rent is due every day.
JJ Watt

WHEN GOD CREATED the planet, one of His best ideas
was the day.

The day begins.
The sun comes up.
It gives light for a little while.
The sun goes down.
During that time, we wake up, we live—we make choices, cre-
ate stuff, and interact with people—and we go back to sleep.
The day ends.

And every morning, we get a new day.

This is how we live our lives: one day at a time. Not one week at a time. Not one month at a time. Not one lifetime at a time. One day at a time. From this perspective, only today matters. If you want to give your life to something significant, steps need to be taken today toward that end.

Say, at the end of your life, you want to be remembered as a generous person. Then, part of your day today must include an act of generosity.

Perhaps you want to be a writer. Well, there's only one question to ask: did you write today?

I know of a lot of guys who want to play in the NFL. If this is you, then how you spend your day today will go a long way in determining if you'll get there.

Annie Dillard says, "How we spend our days is, of course, how we spend our lives."[6] If a large part of your day is watching television or being lazy, then a large part of your life will be the same. But, if you give your day today to perfecting your craft and serving other people, then your life will take the same course.

> *What do you want your life to be about?*
> *How can you incorporate that idea with what you do today?*
> *What will you do with your day today?*

Realizing your God-given potential isn't something you put off until tomorrow. It's what you do today that gets you there.

No Matter What...

The shortest distance between a dream and reality are the choices you make today. Stop living as if you'll live forever. Live today as if it's the first and last day of your life.

Act Like You're Invited

The hand of the diligent will rule,
while the slothful will be put to forced labor.
Proverbs 12:24

Most talented players don't always succeed.
Some don't even make the team.
It's more what's inside.
Brett Favre

ACT LIKE YOU'RE invited, because you are.

An accomplished lawyer, Bob Goff tells a brilliant story about not getting into the law school he wanted to attend. Bob's grades weren't good enough for the school's admittance standards, and no matter what he did, they kept rejecting him. So, Bob decided to participate in a one-man sit-in.

Literally, every day for a week, Bob sat in a chair directly across from the dean of admissions' office, from 9 am to 5 pm. Every morning when the dean arrived at work, Bob was there. When the dean stepped out for a cup of coffee, Bob was there. If the dean left for lunch, Bob was there. And when the dean finally went home at the end of the day, Bob was still there sitting in that chair. This happened for about a week until finally one morning, the dean walked up to Bob and told him to go buy his books. Bob Goff says about the story, "Sometimes, you just have to act like you're invited. Because you are."[7]

If you're an athlete or an artist or really anyone who wants to give something creative to the world, you might feel like there aren't a lot of people asking you to show up, especially if you're new to the game. You might think, *Nobody cares that I'm here*, or *If I don't show up, nobody's going to notice.* Well, let me share a secret with you that I've been tapping into nearly all of my adult life: When you act like you're invited, people begin to believe that you are, yourself included.

To say I was nervous when I became chaplain at Cal Football would be an understatement. I remember going to my first practice and standing in the corner of the end zone alone. I'd only met two or three people. I definitely didn't know my way around. Trying to get into the facility that day, I actually got locked out. Knocking on the door, I felt so embarrassed when the person who opened it looked me square in the eyes and asked, "Who are you?" I felt lost and out of place.

After my third practice of standing in the corner, though, I made a decision. I decided I would no longer go to practices and hide. I was going to act like I was invited.

The next day, I showed up having memorized all the players' jersey numbers. I walked up to some of the guys on the sideline and called them by name. I introduced myself. I asked how they were doing and told them that if they needed anything, I'd be around all season. I started joining the players for dinner a few times a week. I began dropping by the coaches' offices randomly just to see if they needed anything or if I could serve them in any way. Before long, I didn't have to act like I was invited. I was.

The truth is, we're all invited. You're invited, too. If you have a pulse and you're in the room, then God invited you here today. You don't need anyone's permission to give it your all.

Where do you feel intimidated?
Is there anywhere you feel called but not comfortable?
What would it look like for you to begin acting like you are invited?

No Matter What...

When it seems like nobody cares that you're here, all that really means is that you get to surprise people with your presence. Act like you're invited, because you are.

MINDSET

PART THREE

Impossible Is Just a Thought

The simple believe anything, but the
prudent give thought to their steps.
Proverbs 14:15

Doctors and scientists said breaking the four-minute
mile was impossible, that one would die in the attempt.
Thus, when I got up from the track after collapsing
at the finish line, I figured I was dead.
Roger Bannister

WHAT'S IMPOSSIBLE, REALLY?

On May 6th, 1954, Roger Bannister ran and recorded the first
sub 4-minute mile in human history. Until that day, running a
4-minute mile had not only never been done, it was thought an
impossible feat.

The two previous record holders, Swedes Gundor Haag and
Arne Andersson, decided the mile couldn't be run in under 4
minutes. And so, they never did. Their record of 4 minutes and
1 second stood for nearly a decade. John Landy, an Austrian,
who himself ran the mile in 4:02 several times, said the 4-min-
ute mile was "a brick wall" never to be scaled.

The 4-minute mile: impossible, until it wasn't.

On a windy, March afternoon, Roger Bannister broke the iconic 4 minute barrier with a time of 3 minutes 59.4 seconds. A medical student at the time, Bannister simply refused to believe the human body couldn't shave at least a few seconds from the current world record.

He made up his mind that it was possible.
And what his mind decided, his body accomplished.

All the more interesting, just two months later, Landy himself broke the 4 minute barrier. Apparently, the brick wall wasn't as "unscalable" as he originally thought. Once Landy made up his mind that it was possible, his body accommodated.

What we're talking about here is the power of a thought.

Today, the sub-4-minute mile is the standard for middle-distance runners around the world. It's not only possible; it's common, all because one man dared to think differently. He challenged the impossible with a thought.

Some argue that advancements in nutrition or technology, not gains in the human psyche, are the true factors behind growing athletic accomplishments. If that were the case, wouldn't the same phenomenon be occurring among animals? It's not. Take horse racing as an example. Author Steve Chandler points out that thoroughbreds of today aren't any faster than thoroughbreds of 2005, 1995, or even 1955. Despite advancements in nutrition, oxygenation, and training, horses aren't any faster today than they were 60 years ago.[8]

What does this suggest? It's our minds, not our bodies, that push the human race forward.

St. Ignatius said, "Do everything as if God were dwelling in us." In other words, dream a dream that is destined to die without God's intervention. Think bigger. Have the courage to challenge the status quo. Dare to love your enemies. Risk for something you believe in. Work for justice, freedom, and peace. Trust God and go for the impossible.

How many designated impossibilities exist in your life?
What have you deemed impossible that really isn't so?
What different things would you pursue if you actually believed God lived in you?

No Matter What...

Impossible is just a thought. Dare to challenge the status quo. Dream a dream that is destined to die without God's intervention.

Think Differently

The wisdom of the prudent is to give
thought to their ways, but the folly of
fools is deception.
Proverbs 14:8

If everyone is thinking alike,
then somebody isn't thinking.

George S. Patton

IN THE SCRIPTURES, the word *repentance* literally means
to think differently. It means to forfeit one way of thinking in
favor of another.

The great challenge in calling anyone to repentance, though, is
that people don't want to forfeit their current way of thinking.
They see the world the way they do for a reason. Most of us
have been entrenched in a particular way of thinking for years,
if not decades. Changing our minds now is nearly impossible.

Or is it?

Genius, it's said, is the ability to scrutinize the obvious. What
if your going for it isn't just about you getting the most out of

your talent? What if, at the same time, you adopted new ways of thinking? What if you adopted a mindset that encouraged greater levels of commitment, sacrifice, and service to those around you?

There was a defensive player a couple of years back who told me he hated his position coach. He felt as if his coach wasn't giving him a fair shot at playing. To hear him tell it, this coach was a liar, the most negative person on the team, and he didn't care for any of his players. This player said to me, "Kevin, I don't want to feel this way, but I hate him."

It's not uncommon for a player to not like his coach, but to outright hate him? That's a problem. You'll never follow someone you don't respect. You'll never win with a person you choose to hate.

After listening to a few unfortunate stories about this coach, I asked the player how the coach had helped him. I asked him if the coach had ever done anything beneficial for the player. Had he aided the player in any way, ever?

The player said no.

I knew this wasn't the case. I knew the coach had, in fact, given the player a scholarship, coached him at practices, and even recruited him to come to Cal. So, I challenged the player to one week of thinking differently. Instead of going to bed each night and waking up every morning with hate in his heart toward his coach, I asked the player to take one week and pray for God to bless his coach's life.

At first, the player resisted my request, which I understood. Who wants to pray for their enemies, really? But I persisted, and he agreed. For one week, I texted this player daily. I reminded him to take 5 minutes and pray for his coach, to pray that God would bless his coach's family, his work, and anything else he could think of.

A week later, everything had shifted. Not only was the player able to answer my question of how the coach had benefited him, but also he said he no longer hated the man. He didn't necessarily like his coach now, but in praying for him, in making a practice of thinking differently about his coach, the player grew to want good things for his coach's life. He saw his coach with new eyes, less the villain and more a human being.

Where is God inviting you to think differently?
What thoughts do you need to let go of?
What possibilities do you need to open yourself up to?

No Matter What...

You always have a choice as to what you think about a given situation. Have the courage to think differently. Repent and allow God to inform what's true and what's not true.

Stay Positive

A joyful heart is good medicine, but
a crushed spirit dries up the bones.
Proverbs 17:22

If you raise the level of positivity,
then your brain performs significantly better.
Shawn Achor

WHAT VALUE DOES pessimism and negativity add to your life? When has a bad attitude ever served you?

A few years ago, a player approached me who was struggling with depression. He was about to graduate and had no idea what the future held. He'd planned on getting married, but his fiancée called off their engagement. He'd also applied for a few jobs and sought internships, but no one responded. Football wasn't in his future either; he hadn't played a meaningful snap in five years at Cal.

When we sat down to talk, the conversation immediately took a negative turn. He talked about giving up, how he struggled with suicidal thoughts as a kid and similar thoughts were beginning to resurface. Not knowing exactly what to say, I empathized with his concerns and did my best to listen.

And then, in one of those moments where just the right idea reveals itself at just the right time, I reached in my bag and pulled out my journal. Ripping a page from the back, I asked the guy what his football number was—I can't remember exactly what he said, but it was higher than 60. So, I began numbering the page from 1 to whatever his number was. I asked him to tell me all the ways in which God had blessed him. I said we weren't leaving until the page was full. We sat there for probably another hour and a half. It was difficult for him at first, but then, one by one, he began to see. God hadn't abandoned him. In fact, God was everywhere.

Psychologists have discovered that 75 percent of performance and success is linked not to work ethic, not to intelligence or even to talent, but to the level of optimism in your life. Your ability to stay optimistic, to receive encouragement, and to manage stress in a positive way is a better indicator of future success than anything else.[9]

Another study showed that our minds prefer to dwell on negative thoughts over positive ones. When presented with negative information or a threatening situation, our brains attach to such ideas in an instant. Like velcro, we receive the information and instantly fixate on the negative possibilities. Positive information, however, takes, on average, 15 seconds of focused attention to attach to the brain in the same way. For most people, their brains are like teflon to optimism and possibility. This is why taking time to be grateful, to remember your vision, and to see the bigger picture is so important.

God says the same thing in Proverbs 17:22, "A joyful heart is good medicine, but a crushed spirit dries up the bones." Translation: stay positive. Recognize unfortunate circumstances, yes; but, take time to see what else is going on. Allow yourself the opportunity to reconnect to the positive things happening in your life every day.

A few weeks after our first sit-down, I bumped into that player on campus. He saw me from a distance, smiled, and ran over. Giving me a hug, he said, "I want to show you something." Reaching into his back pocket, he pulled out the piece of paper we'd written together. "I read it every morning," he said. "I say a short prayer to say thanks, and then I start my day. It really helps."

You're smarter and more successful when you stay positive.

Where has God blessed you?
What things are going well?
How is God blessing your life today?

No Matter What...

Stay positive. Be optimistic. Smile. Laugh. Hope. This life
is a gift.

Believe in Yourself; God Does

Honor the Lord with your wealth,
with the firstfruits of all your crops.
Proverbs 3:9

The mistake we so often make is thinking
that God's interest and care for us waxes
and wanes according to our spiritual temperature.
Eugene Peterson

BELIEVE IN YOURSELF. *God does.*

If you're a talented player, don't deny it. Embrace your gift.
Make no apology for the hours you put in or the work it requires. Perfect your craft. Use it to serve the people around
you.

If you're a leader, don't be afraid to lead. If you have ideas and
a vision of how things could be, refuse to be timid. Speak up.
Serve the people around you by believing in yourself. Make the
most of this opportunity while you still have it.

It's feels un-Christian of me to invite people to believe in themselves. I was raised in a faith that often hinted to the fact that
I was a worthless piece of crap. The story begins, or so I was

told, with a disclaimer that I suck. I'm a sinner, I'm depraved, everything about me is destined to die, and so on. God provides a Savior, of course, but only after I understand how much of a loser I am and how angry God is over my sin. If anything, according to that version of the story, I shouldn't believe in myself. I should run from myself.

That isn't the original storyline.

That story is just another version of the tit-for-tat, Santa-Claus-god whose biggest concern is punishing you for your sins. That's not the image of Christ we see in the revelation of Jesus.

Jesus looked people squarely in the eyes and said they were the light of the world. He called them "a city on a hill," telling them that if they had faith as small as a mustard seed, they could move mountains. Long before they ever understood the destructive potential of their sin (I'm sure many of them knew already), He told them He believed in them.

> *God believes in you.*
> *You are light.*
> *Shine.*
> *With your talent. In this moment. Shine.*
> *You have so much good to give.*

You're interested in the things you are, in part, because God made you that way. You have the talents, gifts, and opportunities you do because God believes in your ability to steward them for good. God's not mad at you. God doesn't hold a grudge against you. Yes, God invites you to trust God, to live from your true self, and to look to Christ for strength when you need it. God doesn't intend for you to live on your own strength. And...God believes in you.

Nearly all the good God does in the world, God does through people. People like you and people like me, even people who don't know God in the way that I'm writing about now. In the New Testament book of Ephesians, it says God created you to do good things, things God knew you'd do long before you were born, things God hopes you do today to bless those around you.

A mentor of mine once said, "Humility isn't seeing yourself bigger than you are or seeing yourself smaller than you are. Humility is seeing yourself accurately."

If you've got talent, don't deny it.
Be humble, and believe in the talent God's given you.

If you're intelligent, don't deny it.
Be humble, and trust the intelligence God's given you.

If you're a leader, don't deny it.
Be humble, and lead with all diligence.

> *Do you believe in yourself?*
> *How can you begin believing in yourself more today?*

No Matter What...

God believes in you. God believes in your talent. God believes in your passion. God hopes you pursue them with all your heart.

Be Bold, Never Arrogant

When pride comes, then comes disgrace,
but with humility comes wisdom.
Proverbs 11:2

The default mode of the sinful human race
is entitlement, the belief that this gift or experience
that God places in my path is rightfully
mine. I am owed.
John Ortberg

AT THE END of his book, *Big Russ and Me*, the late Tim Russert writes a letter to his son, Luke, that could have come from any father who loves his children. In it, he says,

"Remember, while you are always, always loved, you are never, never entitled. As Grandpa likes to say, 'The world doesn't owe you a favor.'"[10]

I often think of those words when I meet incoming student-athletes at Cal. Brimming with talent and desire, never have I met a player who didn't expect success when he arrived on campus. Unfortunately for many, that expectation is often laced with a small amount of entitlement.

Why do some guys go to class and others don't? Why do certain players make every mandatory meeting, while others make it a regular thing to show up late or not show up at all? Why do some guys give it everything they've got in practice, while others half-ass their way through those same workouts?

The answer to all of these questions is the same: entitlement.

You're entitled whenever you buy into the lie that you're deserving of certain privileges or special treatment over someone else. You're entitled whenever you think certain rules don't apply to you, and that's the way it should be.

This kind of thinking is nothing short of arrogant.

Talent, opportunity, going for it and realizing your God-given potential, these things require you to be bold, but they never warrant you acting entitled. The world doesn't owe you anything. Just because you're you and you're here today doesn't mean you're guaranteed anything tomorrow.

How are you living an entitled life?
What things do you believe you're owed?
The Scriptures say, "Pride comes before a fall." Where are you being prideful?

No Matter What...

Boldness and arrogance aren't the same thing. Step out. Believe in yourself. But, never forget: the world doesn't owe you anything.

Choose Urgency

For the simple are killed by their turning away,
and the complacency of fools destroys them.
Proverbs 1:32

You can be whoever you want to be, you
just have to want it bad enough.
Sparky Anderson

WHAT WOULD IT take for you to live today with a sense of urgency?

God created you with an uncanny ability to respond in crisis. If the building you're in catches fire, and the alarm begins to sound, without hesitation, you could call all of your senses into focus and move.

If the ground beneath you were to begin to shake—this earthquake being the big one—in an instant, you'd drop everything and respond.

The urgency of these moments demands your focused attention, and without trying, you're able to access it. My question is: do you have this ability outside of crisis? Is it possible for you to access this kind of urgency in any moment?

The Scriptures say, "fools are destroyed by their complacency." In other words, smug, self-satisfied people—people who have no need for God and show no respect for the moment at hand—are headed nowhere.

The most successful athletes, coaches and artists don't require crisis to give each day their best. They wake up focused. They live their lives with urgency. They know that hard work beats talent, especially when talent doesn't work as hard.

When was the last time you lived with a sense of urgency?
What did it take for you to live that way?
Is it possible that you haven't realized your God-given potential because you've grown complacent?

The road to failure is often paved with small moments of compromise. Quit living life as if the goal is to kick back and do nothing. Choose urgency. Stop procrastinating.

No Matter What...

You only get one shot at today. Give it your all.

Trust the Process

An anxious heart weighs a man down.
Proverbs 12:25

Sport, like life, is about continuous improvement.
Trust the process.
David Allway

ARE YOU WORRIED or are you concerned? Do you know the difference?

Worry is a state of anxiety, when your mind fixates on trouble or harm. It literally means to tear apart. Worry is paralyzing. Worry is unhelpful. Worry always works against you getting where you need to go.

Concern, on the other hand, is a state of interest. Concern is focused attention on a problem and a potential solution. Concern is creative. Concern is beneficial. Concern often works in favor of you getting where you need to go.

John Wooden won ten national titles, coached UCLA to two undefeated seasons, and at one point, won a record 88 games in a row. Famously, though, he never yelled at his players, waved his arms in the air in panic, or stomped at the refs over a call he didn't like. During games, Wooden remained calm and collected, often sitting quietly at the end of the bench with a program rolled up in his hand as he watched his players play. He said of his coaching style, "If you've prepared thoroughly in practice, the games should take care of themselves."[11]

John Wooden trusted his process. He concerned himself with what needed his attention, and he refused to worry about everything else.

Are you anxious?
Do you find yourself quietly worrying about how things are going to turn out?

God didn't create you to worry. It's not what He wants for your life. Do what you can do today to better yourself and those around you, and then, rest easy. If things don't turn out the way you'd hoped, reevaluate the process and adjust. Whatever you do, stop worrying. It's a waste of energy. It's only tearing you apart.

Stay concerned, and trust the process.

No Matter What...

Worry is wasteful. Concern is creative. Trust the process,
and give God what you can't control.

Pain Is Necessary; Suffering Is Optional

Whoever fears the Lord has a secure
fortress, and for their children it will be a refuge.
Proverbs 14:26

Pain is the rent we pay for being human,
it seems; but suffering is usually optional.
Richard Rohr

IN ORDER TO become a Navy SEAL, a soldier must complete the 6-month Basic Underwater Demolitions/Seal Training (BUDS) course. BUDS is famously the most strenuous and demoralizing training program the US military has to offer. It's designed to challenge both a candidate's physical strength and his mental fortitude. It's a painful experience. With an attrition rate of 75 percent, psychologists have determined that BUDS is almost entirely an exercise in mental toughness.

In his book *Navy Seal Training Guide: Mental Toughness,* Lars Draeger defines what he calls the four pillars of mental toughness: Goal Setting, Mental Visualization, Positive Self-talk, and Arousal Control.[12]

Goal Setting

According to Draeger, goal setting isn't merely making a list of things to accomplish. For a SEAL, breaking down a goal makes all the difference. Micro-goals, short-term goals, mid-term goals, and long-term goals help a soldier keep track of the progress he's making along the way.

For example, if a soldier is asked to run a 90-minute run and follow that up with a 2-mile swim, he might first focus his attention on the run, choosing to set a micro-goal of making it through the first 15 minutes, and then the next 15 and so on until the final 15, before he ever considers the swim. These micro-goals, accompanied with the short-term goal of making it through a single day, are what distinguish a BUDS finisher from a BUDS dropout.

Mental Visualization

Mental Visualization is the practice of seeing oneself complete a task correctly before ever attempting the task itself. Whether it's a technical exercise, a physical challenge, or execution of a mission, a soldier's ability to visualize what and how something needs to be done goes a long way.

Positive Self-talk

Positive Self-talk is the ability to take control of the conversations you allow yourself to have with yourself. Psychologists believe we speak to ourselves anywhere from 500-1,700 words in a given minute throughout the day. This conversation is extremely important in how we approach a task. If we doubt our capacity to realize a goal, we're less likely to achieve it. If, on the other hand, we decide we're capable of the task at hand, we're more likely to realize our goals.

Arousal Control

Arousal Control is a fancy term for controlling your stress levels. SEALS face life-or-death scenarios all the time. Maintaining a low heart rate, the ability to control one's breathing, and remaining calm in tense circumstances prove vital to a soldier's survival. BUDS exposes those candidates who can control their stress levels from those who cannot.

Isn't it true that it's not the circumstances of your life that make you happy or sad; it's what you think about those circumstances that creates those realities?

Everyone faces situations that are painful, but not everyone suffers. Why is that? Because for some people, their thoughts are more powerful than their circumstances. The apostle Paul, one of the most mentally tough figures in all of Scripture, invites us to "Take every thought captive, and make it obedient to God."[13] He invites us to think about things that are true, noble, praiseworthy, and admirable. Regardless of our circumstances, Paul wants us to know that what we think about those circumstances makes all the difference.

God designed you with the incredible capacity to choose what you think about in any given moment. You get to decide your thoughts. Goal setting, mental visualization, positive self-talk, and arousal control are all just exercises in you getting to choose what you want to think about.

What will you spend your time thinking about today?
Your circumstances? Or your commitments?

Pain is necessary; suffering is optional. Your mindset is always more powerful than your circumstances.

No Matter What...

If you're facing a painful situation, you don't have to suffer. Let your thought life dictate how you feel.

At Some Point,
You Just Decide

Hope deferred makes the heart sick,
but a longing fulfilled is a tree of life.
Proverbs 13:12

I was not the fastest player but I was determined
to be the best player I could be on the field.
Jerry Rice

AT SOME POINT, you just decide.

Scott Jurek, a legend in the sport of ultramarathons, has won the Hardrock Hundred (once), the Badwater Ultramarathon (twice), The Spartathlon (3 times), and the Western States 100 Mile Endurance Run (7 times). He's won 35 titles and set 16 course records in 20 years of competition.

In 2010, Jurik set the US record for distance covered in a 24-hour period with 165.7 miles. That's an average of 8 minutes, 42 seconds per mile—for an entire day.

Jurek says of his running, "When people look at it on paper, it doesn't make sense: 'Why do you put your body through all that and your mind?' But I think because in the end, I come out a different person, and I look at life differently."[14]

Jurik says he looks at life differently. He makes a decision, and then he finds a way to accomplish the decision he's made.

Researchers have done studies on ultramarathoners and other elite competitors, including special forces units. They discovered that runners like Jurek produce a disproportionate amount of neuropeptide Y, a molecule that transmits signals in the brain. Literally, Jurek, and others like him, have rewired their brain chemistry to endure pain, overcome obstacles, and just keep going.

Circumstances can be stacked against you. Resources could be lacking. Perhaps your opponent is stronger than you and the naysayers say you don't have a chance. None of that matters, though, if you've made up your mind. Once you decide to act, all of those things become mere details.

The New Testament Scriptures contain eleven letters from the apostle Paul. Four of those letters were written from prison. In Philippians, Paul references joy at least fifteen times. Despite being chained to a prison wall, Paul writes to other Christians and friends spread across the Roman Empire, encouraging them to remain joyful. Imprisoned, in chains, but only joy on his brain: talk about a strong mind. In that letter, he writes, "I know how to get along with humble means, and I also know how to live in prosperity; in any and every circumstance I have learned the secret of being filled and going hungry, both of having abundance and suffering need. I can do all things through Christ who strengthens me..."[15]

In the New Testament, Paul is the ultimate model of mind over matter. At some point, he just decided. From then on, his circumstances no longer determined his fate.

What will it take for you to stop talking about how stacked the cards are against you?
What needs to happen for you to get over all the excuses?
When will you just decide?

No Matter What...

At some point, you just decide. Circumstances are just details. You make up your mind, and you keep going until you get there.

Change Your Mind and Change Your Life

Whoever heeds life-giving correction
will be at home among the wise.
Proverbs 15:31

Asking someone to hold you accountable
is a sneaky way of not taking responsibility
for your life. Instead, be responsible,
and recruit honest friends.
Adrian Koehler

CHANGING YOUR MIND is only half the battle. You have to change your habits if you want to lead a new life.

In May 1971, Congressmen Robert Steele of Connecticut and Morgan Murphy of Illinois returned from a visit to Vietnam with a disturbing realization. Nearly 15 percent of US servicemen in Vietnam were addicted to heroin. The nation was outraged. Within a month, President Nixon announced the creation of the Special Action Office of Drug Abuse Prevention (SAODAP). Its purpose was to fight against drug abuse and addiction, especially within the nation's military.

To this day, SAODAP's work of rehabilitating US Vietnam veterans of heroin abuse stands as the most successful campaign of its kind. No heroin addict was allowed to return to the US until he was determined "dry." Once home, only 5 percent of those veterans ever relapsed. That statistic was at the time, and is today, unprecedented. The average relapse rate among other heroin users treated in the US is 90 percent.

Five percent relapse compared to 90 percent relapse, how can that be?

Jerome Jaffe, the head of Nixon's office of Drug Abuse Addiction, argued it was the change in environment that made all the difference. Jaffe said, "I think that most people accept that the change in the environment, and the fact that the addition occurred in this exotic environment, you know, makes it plausible that the addiction rate would be that much lower."

The addicted Vets had the benefit of working with psychologists and psychiatrists, just like any other addict in rehab. But the Vets also had the added benefit of physically altering the environment in which they lived their lives.

They came home.
Their environment changed.
Every habit changed along with it.

They left Vietnam, and with it, all the familiar rhythms they used to know. In short, they changed both their minds and their habits.

Your brain is wired to do something one way until you rewire it to do it another. What we can learn from the heroin addicts of the Vietnam War is that this rewiring only takes place if you change your habits, if you're able to alter both how you think and what you do.

Richard Rohr says it this way: "You don't think your way into a way of living. You live your way into a new way of thinking."[16]

What habits need to change in your life?
What healthy rhythms can you introduce today?

No Matter What...

Habits eat willpower for breakfast. You can have all the willpower in the world, but you won't change anything until you change what you do.

EXCUSES

PART FOUR

Work Is a Blessing

All hard work brings a profit,
but mere talk leads only to poverty.
Proverbs 14:23

The privilege to work is a gift.
The power to work is a blessing.
The love of work is success.
David Mckay

THERE IS NO secret to success.

The people who succeed in life are the ones who say no to fear, work hard every day, and persevere. It's usually that simple.

Unfortunately for many of us, work isn't something we look forward to. Most people see work as a burden. Work often falls into the category of "Let's get this over with." We prefer leisure, rest, even laziness, to work. Proverbs 14:23 invites us into a new way of living. It says, "All hard work brings a profit, but mere talk leads only to poverty."

Here's how I like to think about this passage: everything worth anything will cost you something. Usually, that something is a lot of hard work.

In my life, God's greatest gifts have been wrapped in work. I've been married eleven years, and I have two children. There are few things in life, if any, that I value more than my family. At the same time, there are few things in my life, if any, that have required more work than my marriage and my two boys. That's just how it goes. Whether it's my job, my writing, my physical health or anything else I value, the more it means to me, the more work it's required.

Elisabeth Elliot says, "The enjoyment of leisure would be nothing if we had only leisure. It is the joy of work well done that enables us to enjoy rest, just as it is the experiences of hunger and thirst that make food and drink such pleasures."[17]

God created work. It was His idea. It's the necessary process by which we realize our potential and achieve our goals. It's also usually how we best serve those around us.

What work has God given you to do this week?
How is the fact that it's difficult a good thing?

Quit complaining about the work you have to do. Do your job, enjoy the work, and receive the reward of having added something valuable to the world.

No Matter What...

Work is a blessing. Whatever God's plan for your life is, I can guarantee you one thing: it involves a lot of hard work.

Risk Is Required

Trust in the Lord with all your heart
and lean not on your own understanding.
Proverbs 3:5

Safe is good for sidewalks and swimming pools,
but life requires risk to get anywhere meaningful.
Simon Sinek

YOU WON'T KNOW until you jump.

You might win.
You might lose.
You could get hurt.
You may burn out.

There's always the outside chance you blow everyone away and become a superstar.

But you won't know until you jump. And jumping means embracing the uncertainty. It means stepping into the unknown and giving it your all.

Risk is required.

I'm always a little conflicted when I pray for the team before we take the field on game day. It's not that I don't want to pray, I do. I just don't think praying for a win is going to win us the game. So, I don't. I never pray for a win. I thank God for the opportunity before us; I pray we'd realize our God-given potential; and I ask for His favor of protection from injury. And, in the back of my mind, I know there's at least one God-fearing athlete on the opposing team praying for the same thing. So, I don't pray for a win.

Winning the game isn't affected by my prayers anyway. It's about the risks you take. It's about whether or not you're willing to jump into the preparation required. It's about whether you'll take the leap and trust your teammates and coaches. It's about your willingness to work hard in season and out of season, waking up each morning and taking the daily leap of faith that your hard work will pay off.

Wouldn't it be great if God mailed us a contract outlining all the costs up front? How much we'd have to sacrifice, what we'd have to endure, and how hard, but temporary, the pain would be along the way? Wouldn't it be great if, in return, God also gave us a peek of all the experiences we'd accumulate, how much we'd gain by trusting Him and persevering, and the kind of person we'd become at the end of this whole deal—stronger, more seasoned, more whole? But that's not how things work. As author Don Miller says, "Some things are for God to know and for us to trust."[18]

You won't know until you jump.

Where is God inviting you to trust Him?
What risks aren't you willing to take today in achieving your goals?
Why not?

No Matter What...

Risk is required. Embrace the uncertainty. Trust God and give it your all.

Size Doesn't Matter

Let not the wise boast of their wisdom
or the strong boast of their strength...
or the rich boast of their riches,
but let the one who boasts boast about this:
that they have the understanding to know me.
Jeremiah 9:23-24

It is not the size of a man but
the size of his heart that matters.
Evander Holyfield

DOUG FLUTIE WAS too small. So was Wes Welker. Steve Smith, Maurice Jones-Drew, Barry Sanders: all undersized. At one time or another, each of these players were told they'd never make it because of their stature.

Size.
Speed.
Ranking.
Conference.

Not one of these things proves who will win and who will lose.

You will never convince me that size decides the outcome. My senior year of high school, I played on an 8-1, top-10 football team in the state of Kansas. Our final regular season game was against our crosstown rival who happened to be the 9-0, reigning state champions. I played right corner, and it was my job to keep outside containment and squeeze every play inside to our all-state linebackers. This was a big task because our opponents led the league in rushing, often utilizing a left sweep to rack up yards.

Much to our advantage, though, our opponents' starting running back, Beno Gore, himself an all-state player, appeared to be injured going into the last game, and they might be forced to play the backup. Watching film, we noticed the backup was tiny. At most, he was 5'6", maybe 130 lbs. I was elated. With such a tiny running back, I figured I was up to the task.

Boy, was I wrong.

It was awful. Not only did I fail to keep outside containment, their backup running back rushed for more yards on us that game than anyone had all season. We lost handily, and I was crushed.

The next season, that backup became their starter. He eventually landed at Kansas State and went on to fame and fortune with the San Diego Chargers, New Orleans Saints, and now, the Philadelphia Eagles. When I played against him in high school, they called him "little tank." Today, this all-pro running back simply goes by his real name: Darren Sproles.

What excuses are you hiding behind?
Are you too small? Are you too young? Are you just a walk-on?
How do you tell yourself the cards are stacked against you?

Quit making excuses. Start proving the haters wrong. Don't boast in your size or lack of it. Boast in the fact that God brought you here, and God will see you through.

No Matter What...

Size doesn't matter. If you're good at making excuses, in time, you'll be good at little else. Trust God, and keep working.

Time Is Never the Issue

The soul of the sluggard craves and
gets nothing, while the soul of
the diligent is richly supplied.
Proverbs 13:4

Action expresses priorities.
Mahatma Gandhi

A MODERN-DAY Renaissance man, my friend Bryan, is above average at everything he does.

Bryan founded and runs a mid-sized, multimillion-dollar tech company—his third such venture. He's also written and published over fifty short stories. He recently wrote his second screenplay, for which he hired real actors and had a table reading in Los Angeles. He's written five opuses, he plays his own music, and he launched a music collective made up of fellow professional writers and musicians. I'm also told Bryan's an excellent cook.

Bryan's the kind of guy who, when you hang out with him, you wonder what you're doing with your own life. How can one man do so much when you have a hard time getting around to cleaning your apartment?

Well, as Bryan would say, time is never the issue.

The reason you never get around to doing certain things in your life is not because you don't have enough time. No, you never "find the time" because the things you're looking to do aren't really priorities. If they were, you'd make time. When you say to yourself, "There's just not enough time," you lie. The truth is, the things that never get done aren't priorities. The things that do get done are.

There's always enough time to do the things God's gifted and called you to do. As Abby McHugh says, "God will not call you to a life you don't have time for."

If I'm honest, many of the things I 'can't find the time for' are actually things I'm afraid of doing. Finishing a writing project, reaching out to a friend I've wronged, or talking to team members about a conflict we're having: in each of these cases, time isn't my issue, a lack of courage is. My priorities are out of whack because of fear.

How about you?
What does what you've accomplished today say about your priorities?
What things aren't getting done that you wish you had more time for?
Why are you so afraid?

No Matter What...

Time is never the issue. Your "time" problem is more likely a courage problem. Quit making excuses. Remember your why. Embrace your fear. Live the life you've been called to live.

Now > Later

Watch your step. Use your head.
Make the most of every chance you get.
Ephesians 5:16

If tomorrow wasn't promised,
what would you give for today?
Ray Lewis

NOW IS ALL you have.

Next week is always a week away.
Next month works the same way.
Now is the only time anything is ever created.

If you look for it, there's always a reason to put off work.

You're busy.
You need more information.
You have more pressing priorities.
You're waiting on someone else.
You aren't sure what to do.
You're not feeling well.
You need a break.
You just have to finish this other thing first.

Isn't it possible, though, that none of these reasons are legitimate, and what's true is that you simply aren't completing the work? Postponing what must happen for "some day" is the surest path to not realizing your full potential. People who wait for "tomorrow" or "once I..." or "when the time is right" know all too well that the required action never comes.

The future isn't real; it's an idea. Action always occurs in the here and now, this present moment. That's why the future is a terrible place to realize your dreams.

Ephesians 5:16 says, "Watch your step. Use your head. Make the most of every chance you get." Translation: You're never going to "get around to it." Do what's required right now, today.

What's the most important action you can take today to realize your vision? What have you been putting off for tomorrow or next week or next month? What's getting in the way of you simply doing what's required?

If you aren't realizing your purpose, it has less to do with how you feel, what your priorities are, who's in the way, how much information you have or don't have, and your energy level. At the end of the day, if the work isn't getting done, you simply aren't doing what's required.

No Matter What...

Now is greater than later. Do what's required right now, and what must happen will always get done.

103

Not Knowing Is No Excuse

And lean not on your own understanding…
Proverbs 3:5

There may be people that have more talent
than you, but there's no excuse for anyone to
work harder than you do.
Derek Jeter

NOT KNOWING IS no excuse.

On May 25, 1961, President John F. Kennedy dared the American people to reach for the stars when he said, "I believe that this nation should commit itself to achieving the goal, before this decade is out, of landing a man on the moon and returning him safely to earth."

At the time, no man or woman had ever walked on the moon. There was no precedent for such a vision. No clear road map for its achievement. No one knew how to do this. No matter. Eight years later, on July 20, 1969, two American astronauts successfully landed on and took mankind's first steps on the moon.

A commitment never hides behind the fact that it doesn't know how to do something.

It reaches out.
It strives anyway.

John F. Kennedy is an example of a man who refused to let what he didn't know keep him from pursuing what he knew must happen.

When I asked Nikki to marry me, I didn't know how to be a great husband. There were plenty of good examples around my life, sure. But I'd never done it myself. That didn't stop me. I was committed; I'd figure it out.

When we moved to Berkeley to plant a church, I didn't have a clue as to what I was doing. Again, that didn't matter. I was committed, and I'd find a way to make it work.

Stop hiding behind the excuse "I don't know how." Find out how. Lean not on your own understanding, and chase down the life God is calling you to live. Go for it.

One more thing, of course you don't know how. You've never done this before. Not knowing how is what makes this an adventure. Lean in. Enjoy the mystery. Find out how and do the impossible.

Is there anything in your life you're not doing because you "don't know how"?

If so, it's not that you don't know how; it's that you're too afraid to try. Be honest with yourself: You're not committed. If you were, not knowing how wouldn't matter. You'd find a way to make it happen.

No Matter What...

Not knowing is no excuse. Failure to act is always an issue of commitment. It's never about a lack of knowledge.

Stop Describing; Start Creating

Do everything without complaining or arguing.
Philippians 2:14

When you blame others, you
give up your power to change.
Robert Anthony

DO YOU DESCRIBE reality? Or do you create it?

A friend of mine likes to make excuses. I'll call this friend me. When I make excuses, I fall into the trap of merely describing things.

> *"It was too hot to run."*
> *"I didn't have enough talent to win the game."*
> *"There were too many injuries to really put together a good team that year."*

Regardless of what reality was true, these excuses allow me the chance to describe why I'm the victim of my circumstances. They prove how I was powerless to do anything other than what I did.

I have another friend who creates things. I'll call him the me I want to be. The me I want to be never wastes his time describing things.

> *"If it's too hot, I'll run in the morning before the heat."*
> *"If I don't have enough talent, I'm going to overprepare and outwork my opponent."*
> *"If some of our first-string guys get injured, we believe in the guys behind them. We'll coach them up and have them as prepared as they can be."*

Again, regardless of what reality actually is, a person who creates things refuses to be the victim of his or her circumstances. The me I want to be is never powerless to act. This me chooses to see every problem as a project and just make it work. If I lose, so be it. But the me I want to be refuses to hide behind excuses.

The great John Wooden defined success not in terms of winning and losing. Rather, success is doing the best you can with what you're given. "Success is peace of mind," he said, "which is a direct result of self-satisfaction in knowing you did your best to become the best you are capable of becoming."

> *Are you describing reality or are you creating it?*
> *Are you making excuses why you can't do something?*
> *Or are you finding reasons why you're going to keep going?*

Stop describing reality. Start creating it. Choose success no matter the outcome.

No Matter What...

You have a decision to make. You can either spend your life describing the world around you or you can commit to creating something new.

What If > What Is

Nothing is impossible with God.
Luke 1:37

You can't depend on your eyes
when your imagination is out of focus.
Mark Twain

TWO WORDS: WHAT and if.

As plain and unassuming as any words in the English language. What and if are as common as they come, that is, until you put them together. When what and if become what if, anything is possible.

In many ways, as a pastor and chaplain, I am a pastor of the what if.

When a person from our church says to me, "I hate my job. My boss is crazy. I'll never be happy here."

I respond with, "What if having a tough boss is the best thing that's ever happened to you? What if this season in your career isn't about what you accomplish professionally as much as it is about who you become personally?"

When a friend approached me a few years ago and said, "My marriage is over. I don't love her. She doesn't love me; we're just not compatible anymore."

I asked, "What if love isn't a feeling you have but a choice you make? What if your marriage isn't over, but it's the dawn of a new season of relationship, understanding and commitment? What if your realizing you and your wife don't love one another is the best thing to have happened to your marriage in decades?"

Perhaps you say to me, "I'm not talented enough," or "My coach doesn't like me," or "I'd be better off somewhere else."

My response to you might go something like this: "What if opportunity is never about talent? What if character is more important?" And "What if your coach not liking you is the best thing that could happen to you? What if knowing that your coach doesn't like you means you no longer have to worry about impressing him or her and you can just focus on getting better?" And "What if somewhere else is no better than right here, right now? Is it possible you don't need new surroundings but a new perspective?"

Unfortunately, most people of faith today are more committed to what is than to what if. Too many people are defined by their beliefs and their creeds, rather than their hopes, dreams, and the visions God's given them. We've become obsessed with certainty when true faith calls us to mystery. Dependence upon God has been replaced with information about God. These two things couldn't be more different.

Where in your life have you settled for what is over what if? Where have you lost hope?

Faith has more to do with what if than it ever did with what is. Refuse to define yourself by what is. Be comfortable with uncertainty. Ask what if in those areas of your life where you've lost hope.

No Matter What...

What if > what is. Faith isn't about certainty but mystery, possibility, and hope.

Purpose > Personality

Appetite is an incentive to work;
Hunger makes you work all the harder.
Proverbs 16:26

It is the set of the sails, not the direction of the wind
that determines which way we will go.
Jim Rohn

I'M NOT A runner.

I don't have a runner's body. I have bad knees. I prefer fast-twitch muscle sports. And in all my life, I never ran long distances competitively at any level. Still, I run. I run because I choose to run.

I'm not a writer. I've never written a book. I didn't study English in college, and I never took a writing class in high school, undergraduate or grad school. But I write. I feel I have something to say. It must be said. So, I write.

Where you came from, your previous experiences, even your personality: these things aren't as important as your purpose.

Maybe you're the first person in your family to go to college. That shouldn't stop you from thriving in this place. Perhaps you've never been challenged at your position. When you were a kid and when you were in high school, you were the best of the best. But here? Here, the competition is fierce. There are a handful of people who are flat out better than you. But that doesn't have to stop you from giving every day your all. These facts don't have to sway your purpose.

Purpose is always more powerful than personality.

Before Walt Disney was Walt Disney, he worked for a local newspaper. The editor told Disney he lacked imagination, had no good ideas, and then he fired him.

Before Oprah Winfrey became "Oprah," she was told she was "unfit for network television," and she was fired from her job as a local TV anchor.

The Beatles first album was rejected. They were told no one "would like their sound" and "guitar music was on its way out."

Theodor Suess Giesel, better known as Dr. Seuss, was rejected by 27 publishing houses before his first book was published.

Refuse to be defined by what other people are looking for. Precedent, preference, personality: none are as powerful as a clearly defined and fully committed purpose.

What are you committed to?
What is your purpose?
Where are you tempted to give in or give up?

No Matter What...

Your purpose is more important than your circumstances and what other people expect of you. Your drive is more potent than others' dissent.

Busy Is Lazy

The Lord will fight for you while you keep still.
Exodus 14:14

The busy person is a lazy person.
Eugene Peterson

BUSYNESS IS LAZINESS.

Our culture's collective obsession with crowded schedules and frantic achievement is not a good thing. Having less margin in one's life isn't noble. Busyness is not a badge of honor and unavailability not a mark of significance.

For one thing, unless you learn to slow down, you'll never seek the silence necessary to see your true self. You'll only hear the noise. The rat-race keeps your eyes cloudy and your life unexamined. If you don't learn to live slowly, you'll keep believing the lie that what you do defines you. Your identity will no longer be something you receive from God; it will slowly morph into something you have to prove to others.

You've done it. I know I have. People greet me, "Hey, Kevin. How's it going?"

I respond, "Busy," with more than a little pride. Sure, my busyness is likely the result of disorganization on my part. I feel busy because, really, I lack vision and have unclear goals, but they don't know that. All they know is that I've got stuff to do, so I seem important.

Unfortunately, another reason we say "busy" is not for pride but due to fear. We tell ourselves we're too busy to pursue the dreams that, deep down, we know God is inviting us into. In reality, we're not too busy, though; we're just too afraid to give it a shot. Indeed, we may have legitimate commitments—class or work or training or a project due. But we always find time for other things. It's just that certain opportunities scare the mess out of us, so we hide behind "I'm too busy."

Stop saying you're too busy. You're not. You either don't have a clear vision for your life, or you're too lazy to take responsibility for that vision. God doesn't call you to a life you'd be too busy to pursue. God doesn't give you dreams you're too busy to reach out for. Be honest with yourself. How you live is what you believe.

You're not too busy to be healthy.
You just like the taste of food that's bad for you more than you care about the health of your body.

You're not too busy to stay in touch with your family.
They're just not as important to you in this season of life as they once were in other seasons.

You're not too busy to pray.
You just don't know how, you're uncomfortable with silence, or you really don't think God hears you.

You're not too busy.
You're probably just lazy or afraid or prideful.
Don't beat yourself up, though. God's not too busy, either. God is patient. God is present. God's grace is ever available to you. Just slow down and be still. Reread the last five sentences. Take a moment, and rest in God.

Do you feel too busy?
What's your vision?
What do you need to quit to realize that vision?
What do you need to make time for to realize that vision?

No Matter What...

Busyness is not a good thing. It's the result of pride, fear, or a vision deficiency. Slow down. Be still. Rest in God.

OTHERS

PART FIVE

Service Is Greater

Many who are first will be last.
Mark 10:31

We know that every moment is a moment of grace,
every hour an offering; not to share them would mean to betray
them. Our lives no longer belong to us alone;
they belong to all those who need us desperately.
Elie Wiesel

IS YOUR VISION big enough?

Few would argue that walking on the moon is an audacious goal. Only twelve men have done it, and it's been nearly 45 years since anyone tried. If either of my boys said to me they wanted to walk on the moon, I'd probably smile and find satisfaction in the fact that at least they're dreaming big. But are they?

Apparently, walking on the moon wasn't a big enough vision for those who did it.

Of the twelve men who graced the lunar surface, many struggled when they returned home. Some became alcoholics, others battled with depression, and a few saw their marriages fall apart. Buzz Aldrin, the second man to walk the moon, left NASA and ended up a used-car salesman in Texas. Not that selling cars is a bad profession, it's not; it's just a far cry from space travel. Neil Armstrong famously got caught up in his own image later in life. He stopped giving autographs because he didn't want people making a profit off his name. He even sued Hallmark for using the phrase "one small step" on a Christmas ornament without his consent.

The struggle many of these men faced is referred to by psychologists as the "lunar syndrome." What do you do with yourself if your biggest dream is realized at age 28? What's next? Say you walk on the moon; how do you follow that act?

It turns out that realizing even your biggest dreams can leave you wanting. Satisfaction isn't guaranteed. So what do you do?

Dream a dream that is bigger than yourself.

Jesus said, "Whoever is first shall be last, and last first." He said, "If you want to find your life, you must lose it in the service of others." He taught that if someone truly wanted to love God, he or she must first choose to love his or her neighbor.

Is your vision big enough?
Does it involve serving anybody other than yourself?

If your vision doesn't somehow involve serving the people around you, it's too small. If you can realize your dream at 18, 19 or 20 and all you did was serve yourself, it's time to dream a bigger dream. You have the talent you have, in large part, because we all need it.

If you're a songwriter, don't write for yourself alone. Write because we all need your music. Write to serve the people around you.

If you're a swimmer, don't swim merely to get Olympic gold. Use your platform to help people. Swim to encourage those who look up to you.

If you're a coach on the rise, don't just work to get the next gig. Coach as a ministry to the players and athletes who look to you for direction. Be a mentor. Use this opportunity to serve others and not just yourself.

Service is the greater vision. Use the gifts God's given you to bless the people around you.

No Matter What...

A vision that only serves yourself is a vision too small. Use your talent to bless people. Whatever opportunity is before you, it's not there just for you. Be a blessing.

Others > Self

Love others as you love yourself.
Mark 12:31

One player's selfish attitude can poison a
locker room and make it hard, if not
impossible, to establish teamwork.
Dean Smith

LEGEND HAS IT that William Booth, the founder of the
Salvation Army, sent the world's first trans-Atlantic telegram.

In December 1910, Booth was unable to attend the Salvation
Army's annual Christmas conference due to sickness. Stuck in
England and unable to travel to the US where the conference
was being held, someone recommended to Booth he instead
send his message via telegram. That way, it could be read to all
those in attendance while he stayed home and got well. Booth
agreed it was a good idea. Telegrams were expensive in those
days, though, so Booth decided to condense his message to
save money. With little effort, he was able to sum up everything
he hoped to convey in a single word:

"Others."

In my seven years as chaplain at the University of California, without exception, every athlete, coach, and support staff, myself included, has needed to hear this message. Others.

Someone once asked Jesus, "Of all the commandments, which is most important?"

He responded, "Love the Lord your God will all your heart, soul, mind, and strength." And He went on, "And the second is like it: 'Love your neighbor as yourself.'"

Jesus wasn't asked what the second most important commandment was, but He offered it anyway. It's almost as if He believed it impossible to obey the first and ignore the second.

For Jesus, it was impossible to love God and not to love other people.

Unfortunately, this comes as a shock to most of us. We struggle to recognize everything isn't about us. I know my default mindset is to wake up into a story only about me. It's my day. It's my life. I work to accomplish my goals. And so, with regularity, I revisit a message I desperately need to hear: Others.

Who has God placed in your life to whom you need to show some love today?

No Matter What...

There are other people in the world. These other people: you need them, and they need you. Others > Self.

Believe in Others; God Does

A heart at peace gives life to the body,
but envy rots the bones.
Proverbs 14:30

It's not the urge to surpass all others at
whatever cost, but the urge to serve others
at whatever cost.
Arthur Ashe

SIX MONTHS AGO, a close friend of mine sat me down and said four words I didn't know I needed to hear. At the time, my life was seemingly going okay. My marriage, my family, the church, Cal football: things were humming along, or so I thought. And then my friend sat me down, looked me square in the eyes, and said these words, "Kevin, we need you."

He went on to say that from his perspective, I wasn't "showing up" in a few areas of my life like I once had. He asked if I agreed, and if so, why? We talked for a while, and then he closed the conversation with five more words that I hadn't heard in a really long time, but I've cherished ever since, "Kevin, I believe in you."

Have you ever had someone tell you they believe in you? It's powerful. Even if you don't believe it yourself, to hear that someone else thinks you're capable equips you with an almost mystical strength.

You have this same capacity to lift the people around you.

In fact, the most important gift you can give your teammates has less to do with how well you perform on the field of play and more to do with how you serve others along the way. I heard a preacher once say, "When God wants to speak to us, He doesn't pass us notes; He usually passes us one another."

Who around you needs encouragement?
Aside from the field of play, why has God placed you around these people in this space?
Do you believe in the people around you? Have you told them?

Quit thinking only of yourself. See the people in your life. Say what you see. Believe in them, and then encourage their work. They'll never be the same.

No Matter What...

Believe in other people. God does. In the same way that God believes in you, God believes in the people around you. Now, go encourage them.

Two Are Better Than One

Two are better than one, because they have
a good return for their labor: If either of them
falls down, one can help the other up. But pity
anyone who falls and has no one to help them up.
Ecclesiastes 4:9-10

Hard work and togetherness. They go hand in
hand. You need the hard work because it's such a
tough atmosphere...to win week in and week out. You
need togetherness because you don't always win,
and you gotta hang tough together.
Tony Dungy

WHAT DOES IT mean to play on a team?

In Genesis 1, the Scriptures tell a story of creation. Each day, God creates, and then it says, "And God saw that it was good." Seven times, it says those very words: "And God saw that it was good." But in Genesis 2, for the first time in human history, God says of His creation, "It is not good..."

Why does God say that?
Because man was alone.

Nobody realizes their full potential on their own. Michael had Scottie. Belichick has Brady. And Jeter played his entire career surrounded by superstars. Individuals may win a game or two, but it takes a team to win a championship.

In the celebrity culture we live in today, the role of the individual is overstated. You are who you are today because of the investment of so many people. You stand on their shoulders. You've needed them every step of the way. You still do.

God created you for community. And the fact that you have a craft you wish to perfect means you'll need other people all the more. If you want to go for this, if you want to go for anything, then you mustn't go alone.

> *Where are you going it alone?*
> *Is there someone you need to reach out to for help?*
> *Is there someone you need to reach out to in order to help them?*

Two are better than one. It is not good for you to go alone. Start depending on your teammates. Trust the people around you. Be there for them, too.

No Matter What...

Be a team player. Trust the people around you.

We > Us & Them

Hatred stirs up conflict,
but love covers over all wrongs.
Proverbs 10:12

The most important measure of how
good a game I played was how much
better I'd made my teammates play.
Bill Russell

"THERE IS NO us and them. There is only us."

Father Gregory Boyle is a Jesuit priest who's spent the last 30 years working with gang members in South Central Los Angeles. In that time, his organization, Homeboy Industries, has employed over 30,000 "homies" in various jobs—at Homeboy Bakery, Homeboy Silkscreen, graffiti cleaning crews, and many other jobs. Homeboy Industries' vision is to assist at-risk and formerly gang-involved youth to become positive and contributing members of society through job placement, training and education.

By any stretch of the imagination, Father Boyle's job hasn't been easy. He buried his first young person due to gang violence in 1988; he buried his 198th in early 2015.

What's crazy about Homeboy Industries' process is that it requires enemies to work side by side. A homie isn't allowed to refuse work just because a fellow employee is from a rival gang. No, if you want to work, you have to work with everyone, even if it means standing shoulder to shoulder with your sworn enemy for nine hours a day, five days a week.

Father Boyle explains that in order to get homies to work together, you must first help them understand, "There is no us and them. There is only us." His work, and the work of Homeboy Industries, is about "dismantling the barriers that divide" and about revealing the mutuality of all people, regardless of neighborhood or affiliation.[19]

When I first started working with student athletes, I had no idea just how competitive the college football landscape really was. As a fan, of course I understood that competition was a part of it. Teams play against other teams; players compete against other players. But it never occurred to me that within every team, competition is ongoing, at every position, all the time. Offense competes with defense. Players compete for playing time. Even the coaches compete with fellow coaches for better coaching opportunities. From my perspective, this presents an incredible challenge to any team that wants to play together. A team divided against itself cannot stand.

Proverbs 10:12 says, "Hatred stirs up conflict, but love covers all wrongs." What this means for you, a competitor hoping to realize a goal, is that even though you compete, your opponent is not your enemy. Your opponent is just your opponent. When the dust settles, you still have more in common with that person or team than you have differences. At some level, you still need them, and they you, especially if your opponent is on your team.

Who is your opponent?
Who is your teammate?
What will it take for you to stop demonizing the other side?
What can you do today to be a better teammate?

If you want to achieve at the highest levels, you have to be okay with competition. You have to be a competitor. But may we never forget that we're stronger together than we are apart. May we always realize our opponents aren't our enemies; they're just our competition.

No Matter What...

Compete, but don't compare. At the end of the day, we is greater than us & them.

Words Have Power

A heart at peace gives life to the
body, but envy rots the bones.
Proverbs 14:30

It's not about you, once you get to this level.
It's not about how many millions you make or
how big your house is or the cars you got. It's
about at the end of the day, what are you going to
do to help your fellow man? Period. What are you
going to do to give back and make a difference
in somebody else's life?
Bo Jackson

I'M CONVINCED WE remember only two kinds of conversations: the ones that discourage us and the ones that lift us
up. Everything else is just talk.

About two years ago, I believe God spoke to me inviting me
to write. In one of those inaudible but undeniable moments,
I sensed God saying, "I have something to say through you;
now go say it." So, what did I do? I wrote. No, I didn't write a
book or start a blog or anything like that. Instead, I decided the
best way for me to begin writing was to encourage people in
and around my life with handwritten notes. In fact, I set a goal

on January 1, 2014, to write one note a day for the whole year to anyone I believed needed encouragement that day. Now, I didn't actually realize my goal, but that year I did write over 200 handwritten notes to encourage people. The response I got was overwhelming.

Not one person said they'd wished I hadn't written them.

I encouraged couples on their wedding day. I encouraged new parents on the day of their child's birth. I encouraged at least a dozen people the week after they lost a job. I wrote one difficult but encouraging letter to a family grieving the loss of their 26-year-old daughter.

I wrote notes to several people struggling through depression and sadness. I wrote at least 100 notes to various people just telling them something I admired about them. I wrote notes to friends and family. I wrote notes to strangers. And although I didn't write every day, every day I did write, the note was always well received.

One unique thing I did during this project was that I chose to write to people I didn't really know but knew of. If I decided they needed encouragement, I'd just write.

On one such occasion, I wrote a note of encouragement to an influential community leader who'd recently lost her job in an unfortunate, public fashion. I'd met her only a handful of times, and we didn't know one another well. I'm not sure she even knew my name. That said, the week she lost her job, I sat down and wrote her a two-page note telling her everything she'd done well.

In my letter, I wrote and told her that from my perspective, she'd added great value to the whole Bay Area by the work that she'd done. I thanked her for her creativity and her leadership. The day I dropped the letter off with her secretary, I figured that was the end of it. We didn't know one another well. We did have mutual friends, and I'd given her my number in the letter, but I never expected to hear anything else about it.

And then, in a conversation with a mutual friend some months later, I found out the recipient of my letter had been carrying the note around in her purse. For weeks, when certain people would ask her how she was doing, she'd respond by pulling out my letter and say she was doing okay, at least in part, because of the letter in her hand.

I was blown away. All I did was take about 15-20 minutes and jot down some thoughts I had on her situation. Little did I know it was going to actually have an impact on her life. I had no clue she'd carry my letter around with her like that.

That's when it hit me. When you encourage other people, you give courage away.

Courage is difficult for many of us to muster up ourselves. But when we take the time to encourage others, it's like we're giving courage away for free. In the case of this woman, she was carrying my note around in her purse because, for her, it was like carrying courage in her pocket.

Your words have tremendous power. Lift up those around you.

Who can you encourage with words today?
Who needs help? Have you reached out?

No Matter What...

Words shape life. Be picky about what you say. Don't waste your words on just talking. Use them to give courage away.

Correction > Compliment

Wounds from a friend are better than kisses from an enemy.
Proverbs 27:6

I desperately want to be coached.
Aaron Rodgers

PEOPLE DO ONE of three things when offered the truth: they rise up, they hold back, or they run like hell.

Who doesn't love a good compliment? Seriously, think about the last time someone pulled you aside and praised you. Didn't it feel good?

"Great game."
"You were amazing out there."
"I don't think I've ever seen someone do what you did today. Great job."

Compliments are important. They fuel the fire. They affirm the work. They help you believe this whole thing is worth it. But do you feel the same way about correction? If someone were to walk up to you today and offer advice, even a rebuke, how would you feel?

"That was not your best game."
"Hey, you're not doing this correctly. Try it this way."
"Your attitude needs to change. You need to be a better teammate."

Correction isn't always welcome. It can be uncomfortable. It can be deflating. It can lead you to question the work. But great things never come from comfort zones. Facts don't care about your feelings. If something is true and you don't see it, don't you need someone to tell you about it? If results are the goal, isn't it better to receive truthful correction than flattering compliment?

Proverbs 27:6 says, "Wounds from a friend are better than kisses from an enemy." It is better to receive the uncomfortable, deflating, open-to-interpretation correction from someone who cares about you than it is to get random praise from strangers.

What will you do with the truth today: will you rise up or will you hold back?
Will you receive correction from a coach or a mentor or a teammate? Or will you run like hell?

The flip side of Proverbs 27:6 is also worth paying attention to today. Friends tell the truth, even if that truth is going to sting someone they love. This takes practice and wisdom, but you shouldn't be afraid to tell the uncomfortable truth to the people you love. Sometimes, it's how you love them best.

No Matter What...

Correction > Compliment. Welcome the feedback of others. Don't be afraid to tell the truth when necessary.

Actions Power Words

Don't just listen to God's word. You must do what it says.
Otherwise, you are only fooling yourselves.
James 1:22

Well done is better than well said.
Benjamin Franklin

YOU ARE YOUR words and your deeds.

What we say and what we do is how we know anybody. It's our words and deeds that shape our reputation, outline our influence, and facilitate our ability to change a given situation. Let me say it another way: if you're going to go for it, the only real resources you have are your words and your deeds.

There's an old story about a guy who falls into a pit. The pit is so deep and the walls so steep, he can't get out. A priest walks by, and the guys shouts, "Hey Father, can you help me?" The priest writes out a prayer, throws it down in the pit, and he keeps walking. Then a doctor passes by, and the guy shouts up, "Hey doc, can you help me? I'm stuck down here." The doctor writes out a prescription and throws it down into the pit, and he keeps walking. Finally, a friend walks by, "Hey Joe, it's me.

I'm stuck down here, can you help me?" And the friend jumps down into the pit. The man immediately says, "Are you stupid? Now we're both down in this pit."

The friend replies, "Yeah, but I've been down here before, and I know the way out."[20]

Three passersby, all of whom offered words, the priest a prayer, the doctor a prescription, but it was the friend who offered both words and deeds that actually helped the guy out.

You are not your words or your deeds. You are your words and your deeds; the two were never meant to be separated. It's one thing to say you care. It's a whole other deal to act out your care, to meet someone's need by helping them out of the pit.

What words did you speak today? What did they create?
In terms of the people around you, are your words being used to build people up or to tear them down?
Do your actions follow what's being said?

The tricky thing about words and deeds being the foundation for reputation, influence, and impact is that we can fool one another into thinking we're doing something we're not. When what we say isn't in line with what we do, we lie. We're of no help to anybody, including ourselves.

James 1:22 says, "Don't just listen to God's word. Do what it says. Otherwise, you're fooling yourself." James wants us to know that how we live is really what we believe. You can know every Scripture passage in the Bible, have every creed memorized and every prayer recited, but if your words don't match your actions, you're a fraud.

What can you do today to back up what you've said?
How can you better live out your beliefs?

No Matter What...

Actions power words. What you say is so important, and it's what you do that proves your true commitments.

Slow Down and See

They have eyes but do not see...
Jeremiah 5:21

It's not what you look at that matters,
it's what you see.
Henry David Thoreau

DO YOU SEE the people around you?

In 1973, a Princeton University study showed that people in a hurry are less likely to help others. In the study, seminary students were asked to fill out questionnaires about their beliefs. They were also asked to prepare a short sermon, some on various topics concerning religion and others specifically on the parable of the good Samaritan, a story about a priest and a Levite passing an injured man on the roadside before a Samaritan comes along and helps the man. After each student completed the questionnaire, they were told to walk to another building on campus to give their sermon.

To one group of students, the researchers said, "You'd better hurry. You're running late for the next thing." To another group, they said, "You've got plenty of time, but you should probably head over anyway."

This is where it gets fun.

The researchers hired an actor to play a man in need, not unlike the man in the story of the good Samaritan. The actor was positioned so that every student would encounter the man along the way to the next building. The researchers wanted to see who would stop and help and who wouldn't.

The results?

In "low hurry" situations, 63 percent of the students stopped to help the man. In "high hurry" situations, only 10 percnet of the students stopped to help. It didn't matter if the students had just studied the story of the good Samaritan or not. The only determining factor in whether or not a student was willing to stop was if he or she was in a hurry. The study said, "Some (students) literally stepped over the victim on their way to the next building!"[21]

You get the point: don't be in such a hurry.
Slow down.

Theologian and author Dallas Willard says, "We must ruthlessly eliminate hurry from our life, for hurry is the great enemy of spiritual life in our world today."

Are you in a hurry?
Why?
When will you slow down?
Who have you stepped over that you probably should have stopped to help?

Be quick, move fast, but learn to live slowly. Take time today to see the people around you.

No Matter What...

You can't help people if you're always in a hurry. Slow down. See. Reach out.

People Matter Most

No one has ever seen God; but if we love one another,
God lives in us and his love is made complete in us.
1 John 4:12

I have written so many books on God,
but after all that, what do I really know?
I think, in the end, God is the person you're
talking to, the one right in front of you.
Leon Dufour

EVERYTHING MATTERS, BUT people matter most.

Know why. Set goals. Make a plan. Measure your days. Work is a blessing. Risk is required. Size doesn't matter. Stop describing and start creating. Think differently. Stay positive. Choose urgency, and trust the process. And on and on.

These things matter.
But people always matter most.

This is bigger than you. This moment, these talents, what you do with the opportunity in front of you: it's the people in and around this moment that give it its value. You belong here, with them, and they with you. You are not alone in this, and that's why it's so meaningful.

Social psychologists have shown that a sense of belonging is tied to so many things: motivation, happiness, health, and perseverance. Being a part of a community raises your IQ, improves your immune system, and gives you more self-control. But you don't need a study to be reminded of what you already know. Life is about relationships. Being loved and loving someone else is what gives life meaning.

Why should it be any different with your talent?

You may not play a team sport. You may be a golfer, play tennis, or run track. You may swim or throw or surf. But life is always a team sport. You've needed encouragement and coaching and support to get where you are today. And people have needed you in return—your advice and friendship and love. So, don't be afraid to belong. Work on your craft, yes, but keep reaching out to the people around you.

First John 4:12 says, "If we love one another, God lives in us." Think about how simple that is: if you love somebody, God lives in you. No secret prayer, no complicated theology, just a single act of love and you can experience the God of the universe. A lot of people struggle to know and understand God, but loving God is easy: just love your neighbor.

Who are the people who make this so important?
How can you better belong in this place with these people?
What act of love can you offer a friend or teammate today?

No Matter What...

Everything matters, but the relationships in and around
your life always matter most.

COMMITMENT

PART SIX

Stop Saying Should; Start Saying Must

A farmer too lazy to plant in the
spring has nothing to harvest in the fall.
Proverbs 20:4

People almost never do what they
think that they should do. But they
always do what they feel they must do.
Dusan Djukich

STOP SHOULD-ING ALL over yourself. Decide what must happen, and only do it.

In August 2012, the BBC published a series of articles they called "Epic Time-Wasting." The articles told stories of people's outrageous bouts with procrastination.

Caroline of Wirral, England, wrote, "I started decorating the bathroom in 2000 when I moved into this house. The tins of paint are still on display 12 years later, and the work awaits completion."

Ian wrote about his friend Dave, saying, "He would do anything to avoid (his work). At one point, he infamously found himself weighing the cat, convinced that he would only be able to settle down to work if he had the data (on) hand."

Steve from Hampshire said, "When we first got married, my wife brought home a whiteboard on which we could list the jobs that needed to be done. About a year later it disappeared. Just before our silver wedding anniversary (25 years), I found the whiteboard in our garage. There were about 20 jobs on it. None of them had been done—and most of them still needed to be done."[21]

You'll never achieve your full potential living in a world of could and should. You have to decide what must happen and do that thing.

At the beginning of every week, I sit down and make a few lists. The first is a meal plan. It includes the meals we'll eat during the week and the groceries we'll need. The second is a list of people I'm committed to serving. The "committed to serving" list is exactly what it sounds like, a list of people I aim to serve in the next 5-7 days. I like to write notes and encourage people. The final list is a "what must happen" list. The "what must happen" list is not a to-do list. It's not a list of tasks I should get done if time allows. It's not grouping of items I could do. No, the "what must happen" list contains all the things that will get done, no matter what, in the week ahead.

There's a world of difference between could or should and must.

You probably should drink more water than you do. But you must have at least a little water every day to survive.

You could find the most comfortable, spacious place to live in the world and go live there. But you must have somewhere to sleep tonight.

You could be the best-dressed person on the team. But you must find something to wear before you leave the house each morning.

The same is true for your sport. You could work harder today, stay a bit more focused, or be a better teammate, even a little. You probably should do these things. But until the coulds and shoulds in your life become musts, realizing your vision is still just optional. Stop fooling yourself. What could and should happen aren't as important to you as what you're absolutely going to do.

What must happen in your life today?
What things continually show up on your to-do list but never get accomplished?

No Matter What...

Stop saying should. Start saying must. Only focus on what must happen.

Commitments > Circumstances

Commit to the LORD whatever you do,
and he will establish your plans.
Proverbs 16:3

To hell with circumstances;
I create opportunities.
Bruce Lee

A GOOD FRIEND recently asked me if I thought I could raise 5 million dollars in a week. I told him no, probably not. I had experience raising funds, but 5 million dollars was a lot of money. I said I didn't think it was possible for me, especially in only a week's time.

My friend then told me it wasn't a matter of possibility or impossibility. He said it was a matter of commitment.

Rephrasing the question, he asked me if I thought I could raise 5 million dollars in a week, adding the qualifier that if I didn't raise the money, my son Zander would be denied an emergency life-saving surgery. This time, my answer changed. Yes, I could raise 5 million dollars in a week. To save my son's life, I'd make it happen.

The lesson of my friend's questioning was this: Commitments > circumstances.

What you achieve in life, and the fruit you enjoy along the way, have little to do with your circumstances and everything to do with your commitments. When you're committed to something, circumstances won't stop you. They'll just make the journey more interesting. Commitments are always greater than circumstances.

> *Commitments embrace obstacles.*
> *Commitments endure critics.*
> *Commitments weather success, failure, injury, and worse.*

Proverbs 16:3 says, "Commit to the Lord whatever you do, and he will establish your plans." This proverb invites you to take your commitments even one step further: have commitments, yes, but then commit your commitments to the Lord. Pursue them with gratitude, humility, grace, faithfulness, honesty, and perseverance. This is what it looks like to trust God. If you do these things, circumstances won't dictate the outcome of your efforts; God will.

> *What are you absolutely committed to in your life?*
> *Do you pay more attention to your circumstances or to your commitments?*
> *How can you better commit your commitments to God today?*

No Matter What...

Commitments > Circumstances. Commit. Quit complaining. Stop hesitating. Make no excuses. Live a no-matter-what kind of life today.

Decisive Action > Confidence

Slack habits and sloppy work
are as bad as vandalism.
Proverbs 18:9

I prayed for twenty years but received
no answer until I prayed with my legs.
Frederick Douglass

MOST OF MY best decisions were decisions I lacked the confidence to make.

The decision to ask my wife to marry me: I was 60 percent confident. Any guy who says he was 100 percent confident when he proposed is lying. Of course, my lack of confidence had less to do with her and more to do with me.

The decision to start pastoring a church: I was 35 percent confident. I was 26 years old; I had no experience. I was in a new town, with new people, and I had only a few friends in the area.

The decision to grow our family: I was 70 percent confident. I've always wanted to be a father, but that didn't mean I was ready. It's one of the surest things I've ever done, but still, deciding to have children was a whole new ball game for me.

The decision to write: I'm 38 percent confident. Can I write? Will anyone listen? What if people disagree with what I have to say? At the moment, I'm choosing not to care about any of that. I feel as if I have something to say, so I write.

Confidence comes and goes. We'd all like more of it, but we don't need it. We don't need confidence to act any more than we need a straw to drink. It's nice, but unnecessary. To get where God invites us to go, all we need is decisive action.

Too many people get caught up in asking what God's will for their life is. We lack the confidence to choose, so we hide behind waiting on what we think God wants for us to do. When we do this, we're not really waiting on God. Let's be honest; we're hiding in fear.

Decisive action > confidence.

Do you want to know God's will for your life? Make a choice. Choose action over inaction, and see where God shows up.

In the end, God cares more about who you're becoming and how you live today than where it is you go anyway. So, decide. Act. Make a choice, confident or not, and see where God takes you.

Where do you lack the confidence to move forward?
Do you really need confidence? Or do you just need to make a decision?
Is it possible God doesn't want you to be confident right now so you'll learn to trust Him?

No Matter What...

We can have all the confidence in the world, but until we choose to act, we go nowhere.

You're Either All In or Not In at All

Trust in the Lord with all...
Proverbs 3:5

If you aren't going all in,
why go at all?
Joe Namath

RETREAT IS EASY when given the option.

In 1519, Spanish Captain Hernán Cortés landed on the coast of Veracruz to begin what would become Spain's conquest of the Aztec people. Once on shore, Cortés ordered all 11 ships that brought he and his men across the sea to be burned. Legend has it, one of Cortés' men laughed out loud at the request as if to say, "Burn the ships? Are you crazy? You must be joking."

With no hesitation, Captain Cortés drew his sword and stabbed the man in the chest, killing him on the spot. No one dared question Cortés again. The fleet of ships was burned immediately.

The story of Captain Hernán Cortés is a story of commitment. The only thing Cortés wanted his men thinking about was advance. He burned the ships so that the men had nowhere to retreat. He wanted them all in or not in at all.

Proverbs 3:5 is a Scripture often referenced in sports circles. "Trust in the Lord with all your heart and lean not on your own understanding. In all your ways acknowledge Him, and He will make your paths straight." Now, there are many different ways to understand this passage and apply it to our lives. But in every teaching, one thing mustn't be overlooked: the word *all*.

Proverbs 3:5 does not say, "Trust in the Lord with some of your heart." It doesn't say, "In most of your ways acknowledge him." No, it says all. With all your heart. In all your ways.

I often wonder why more of my paths aren't straight. Why am I confused? Why do I get frustrated? Why do I complain so much? The answer is simple. I'm only half-committed. My faith is weak because I trust God with only some of my life.

Burn the ships.
Go all in.

Trust God will all your heart, and see what God does with your path. If you want more faith, trust God with more of yourself. If you want more fruit in your life, don't water the tree half as much. Give it everything.

What would it look like for you to go all in today?
Where have you only been giving some or most of your heart?
What ships do you need to burn so that your focus is only on what's ahead of you?

Giving 75 percent in practice will never translate to you realizing 100 percent of your potential on game day. Go all in today.

No Matter What...

Know that God sees more than you see. If you're going to trust God with anything, trust God with everything. You're either all in or you're not in at all.

Comfort Is a Horrible Goal

Consider it a sheer gift, friends, when tests
and challenges come at you from all sides.
James 1:4

You can be comfortable or
courageous, but you cannot be both.
Brene Brown

REALIZING GOD-GIVEN potential isn't rocket science; it takes what it takes. More often than not, it takes a willingness to keep stepping out, to keep pushing yourself past the limits of your own comfort.

Scientists recently proved that the old adage "No pain, no gain" is true. Researchers at the Scripps Research Institute in Florida studying the biochemistry of the sympathetic nervous system concluded that more intense exercise changes the body at a molecular level in ways that easier workouts cannot. The study discovered that more intense workouts triggered the sympathetic nervous system to release catecholamines and the protein CRTC2 at greater levels than milder workouts, resulting in tighter, stronger muscles.

In other words, they proved that when you push yourself, you improve yourself. They also proved that if you don't push yourself, you stay the same.

Who likes pain? I mean really, who likes pushing themselves past the point of exhaustion? People who want to get stronger, that's who. Arnold Glasow says, "Success isn't a result of spontaneous combustion. You must set yourself on fire."

If you want to be faithful to the things God's calling you to, you can't be afraid of being uncomfortable. What works and what's easy are rarely the same. Stop looking for shortcuts. Quit holding out for an easier way. Comfort isn't the goal.

Too often, I find myself looking for a break, for a chance to take it easy or to find a shortcut. How about you? But when I take a step back and look over my life and my purpose—being a faithful husband, a good father, a loving pastor, and more—I remember comfort isn't my goal. I'm not looking for comfort; I'm longing for impact. James 1:4 goes as far as to say being uncomfortable is a gift from God. We should consider trials and challenges and moments we're forced to persevere as good things.

At the end of a workout, are you spent? Have you emptied the tank of what you can give?
If so, you're on the right track. If not, why not?
Remaining comfortable won't get you anywhere new.
What pain do you need to keep enduring in order to grow?
How can you push yourself a little further today?

No Matter What...

Push yourself past the level of your own comfort. Choose intensity. Set yourself on fire, so to speak, and get somewhere new.

The Footnotes Make the Headlines

All hard work brings a profit,
but mere talk leads only to poverty.
Proverbs 14:23

The fight is won or lost far away from witnesses—
behind the lines, in the gym, and out there on the road,
long before I dance under those lights.
Muhammad Ali

WHAT FOOTNOTES DOES today hold?

Footnotes mostly go unnoticed. They live at the bottom of the page, sometimes at the back of the book. Their print is small, as to not distract from the story and, especially, the headline. The truth is, though, if there were no footnotes, there'd be no headlines.

The headlines of Super Bowl XLI read,
"Super! MVP Manning, Indy Win First Title" and
"Champs! Colts Win Indy's First Super Bowl."

The storyline of the game, however, was the rain.

In the wet conditions, Chicago's quarterback, Rex Grossman, struggled throughout the game to hold on to the football. He fumbled twice and threw two interceptions. His counterpart, Peyton Manning, never fumbled. Asked after the game why the rain didn't seem to be a factor, Manning's center, Jeff Saturday, said Manning regularly practiced snapping and throwing with water-soaked footballs. Although his team plays half its games in a dome, Peyton Manning did this every week because he wanted to be prepared for anything.

Headline: "Colts Win Super Bowl, Manning MVP."
Footnote: Peyton Manning, despite playing most of his games indoors, demanded to practice a few times every week, all season long, with wet footballs.

Proverbs 14:23 says, "All hard work brings a profit, but mere talk tends only to poverty." The first half of that proverb is the footnote. You do the hard work before the profit shows up. Pastor Mark Batterson says, "If you do the little things like they're big things, God will do big things like they're little things." Doing the small things well, finishing the workout with the same intensity you started, going to class and paying attention, studying everything you can in the film room—these are the footnotes of a successful student-athlete.

What small things are required of you today?
Are there any seemingly unimportant details that could use your attention?

No Matter What...

Quit talking about the headlines; keep working on the footnotes. The footnotes make the headlines possible. Day in,
day out, year after year of footnotes, and one day, you'll
wake up to a headline.

COMMITMENT: Hesitate and You'll Hurt Yourself

Hesitate and You'll Hurt Yourself

Have no fear of sudden disaster or of the ruin that
overtakes the wicked, for the Lord will be at your side
and will keep your foot from being snared.
Proverbs 3:25-26

Believe you can and you're halfway there.
Teddy Roosevelt

DO YOU KNOW who won the pro bowl last year?

Me neither. No one does. No one cares.

Nobody cares about the NFL Pro Bowl because it's a game
played at half-speed, the result of which means nothing.

The same is true of us. When we live our lives halfheartedly, as
if our actions don't matter, thinking our contributions are of
no significance, we're forgotten. Worse, we make no difference
in the lives of those around us.

My friend Dave is a life coach, and he likes to get in my face
about this very issue. He keeps telling me I'm hesitating. He

says I too often live my life relying on talent alone, that I'm reluctant to risk and put myself out there. He says my hesitation isn't just hurting me; it hurts everyone around me.

As a kid, I had a coach who said I was more likely to get hurt if I played timidly, going 75 percent or 80 percent. He said it's better to go 100 percent in the wrong direction than 75 percent the right way. I don't know if that's true or not, but I do know I wasn't created to live my life half-heartedly.

Where are you hesitating?
Why are you timid?
What are you afraid is going to happen?

Dave says the greatest issue surrounding my hesitation is that it's so self-centered. I hesitate because I'm only thinking of myself, how I'll fail or what might happen to my reputation. He says if I kept the most important thing the most important thing, namely, how my actions will serve the people around me, it shouldn't matter what happens to me along the way.

No Matter What...

God created you to go for it. He didn't give you a spirit of timidity, but of power. Hesitate, and you won't just be hurting yourself; you'll be hurting us all.

Expect Greatness

The LORD is good to those who wait for him,
to the soul who seeks him.
Lamentations 3:25

You must expect great things of
yourself before you can do them.
Michael Jordan

EXPECTATIONS ARE EVERYTHING.

As the senior leader of a church, it's my job to set expectations for our staff, the board of directors, and all the leaders spread across our community. Usually, if there's a conflict within the church, it's not about something that happened; it's about what people expected to happen and didn't. The conflict isn't circumstantial. It's perceptual. This principle applies to nearly every arena of life.

If my wife and I get into a fight, 99 percent of the time, we don't fight about what happened. Our conflict is about what she or I expected to happen and didn't.

If you begin a season with the expectation of being a starter and contributing, but you never get off the bench, your struggle won't be with what actually happened on the field. Your greater struggle will be an internal one, with your expectations going unmet.

I'd like to invite you to a lofty expectation: greatness. I invite you to expect greatness from yourself this season. Now, by greatness, I'm not talking about wins and losses. I'm not talking about Heisman trophies or you becoming a first team All-American. I'm not even talking about playing time or moving up the depth chart.

Jesus talked about expectations quite a bit and in the most counterintuitive ways. He said if we wanted to be great, we should look for opportunities to become less. We should expect greatness to come not from having the best seat in the room or from receiving the praise of other people. No, Jesus said greatness comes from giving up our seat to those that don't have one and by letting our acts of kindness go unnoticed. His life modeled this expectation. He lived a great life by noticing those on the margins, by loving the unlovable, by washing His disciples' feet, and ultimately, by laying down His life for everyone around Him, friend and enemy alike.

Greatness is not success, not by the world's standards anyway.

Greatness is not fame. Greatness is not fortune. Greatness isn't coming out on top. Greatness, according to Jesus, is serving the people around you. It's considering others better than yourself. Greatness is giving your life away to those who need help, need encouragement, and need you to be more than just some player who stands out from everyone else.

And so, I invite you to expect greatness. Expect opportunities to serve others. Look for ways to be humble and to help other players and coaches who need you. Don't worry about going unnoticed. Serving is more important than being praised.

How can you serve someone other than yourself today?
What great things can you expect from yourself this week?

I think it's fine to expect yourself to perform at a high level; I encourage that, too. But if you expect true greatness, you'll never be disappointed with the many opportunities God gives you. If you pay attention, within every moment, there is a chance to serve somebody.

No Matter What...

Greatness often looks like loyalty, patience, service, humility, honesty and kindness. Be great today. Anticipate opportunities to show your greatness to others.

Everything Worth Anything Will Cost You Something

Those who work their land will have
abundant food, but those who chase
fantasies have no sense.
Proverbs 12:11

Today I will do what others won't,
so tomorrow I can accomplish what others can't.
Jerry Rice

JERRY RICE IS widely considered the greatest receiver
in NFL history. Winner of three super bowls, the 13-time
pro-bowler holds records for most receptions, most receiving
yards, and the most touchdowns in an NFL career. His was a
once-in-a-generation kind of talent. If you could talk to his
teammates, though, they'd tell you it wasn't Rice's talent that
led to his success. His work ethic was second to none.

In his book, *Talent Is Overrated*, Geoff Colvin highlights Rice's
work ethic, saying:

> "In team workouts he was famous for his hustle;
> while many receivers would trot back to the quar-

terback after catching a pass, Rice would sprint to the end zone after each reception. He would typically continue practicing long after the rest of the team had gone home. Most remarkable were his six-days-a-week off-season workouts, which he conducted entirely on his own. Mornings were devoted to cardiovascular work, running a hilly five-mile trail; he would reportedly run ten forty-meter wind sprints up the steepest part. In the afternoons he did equally strenuous weight training. These workouts became legendary as the most demanding in the league, and other players would sometimes join Rice just to see what it was like. Some of them got sick before the day was over."[22]

Hustle.
Sprints.
Extra practice.
Off-season work.
Mornings.
Demanding runs.
Legendary workouts.

Jerry Rice didn't become the iconic figure we all know him to be because he had more talent than the next guy. Jerry Rice became Jerry Rice because he paid a price other guys weren't willing to pay. His story highlights one of life's penultimate truths: the things we value most will demand the most of us.

A good education.
Sounds great, but you'll have to work for it. They don't hand out diplomas to just anybody.

A happy marriage.
I want one, but it's among the most self-sacrificial commitments I've ever made.

A fruitful career.
Yes please, however the marketplace is oversaturated, the economy is fickle, and there are ten thousand other applicants just as qualified as you. Work is required.

Healthy kids and a happy family.
Of course, but first diapers, then toddlers, teenagers, and 20-plus years of being on-call and paying for everything along the way.

Everything worth anything will cost you something. So, resist your urge to complain about how tired you are. Quit thinking about how difficult this is. Decide to enjoy the price of it all. The fact that this is difficult, the reality that it costs you something, means it's worth something.

How much is this dream costing you?
Do you know why?

Think about your time, your energy, your body, and your sacrifices. Now, stop and thank God for how much this costs. Remember, the more valuable it is, the more it will cost you along the way. Your talent isn't the price you pay; the work you're willing to put in is.

No Matter What...

Everything worth anything will cost you something. Pay the price and receive your reward.

Some Things Come to Pass

Discretion will protect you, and
understanding will guard you.
Proverbs 2:11

You will find that it is necessary to let
things go, simply for the reason that they are heavy.
C. Joybell

I HAD A lady once tell me that her favorite passage of Scripture was the phrase "and it came to pass." Confused, I looked it up.

"And it came to pass" appears in the Bible over 1,200 times. Perhaps its most famous occurrence is at the beginning of the traditional reading of the Christmas story in Luke 2: "And it came to pass that in those days, Caesar Augustus issued a decree…"

Honestly, when I hear "and it came to pass," I think of "once upon a time" or something along those lines. That's not what it means. "And it came to pass" is a double entendre, meaning it's a figure of speech that can be understood in two ways.

The first meaning has to do with time. Some seasons come our way, but they only stay for a short while. When they end, and they all do, so will the opportunities associated with them. Defining the phrase this way, one might use "and it came to pass" to introduce the start of a particular season and highlight its uniqueness or value.

And it came to pass that you're a D1 athlete or coach. There never has been and there never will be another time in your life quite like this one. So, enjoy it. Savor everything. Accumulate as many experiences as you can today because this season will pass.

The second meaning of "and it came to pass" also has to do with time, but it's not about the novelty of the season. In this case, "and it came to pass" refers to something within the season that is just passing through, if not gone already. This meaning usually refers to a struggle you've had to endure. It could be an injury, a problematic relationship, or a losing season. The struggle came, but it came to pass. In this case, "and it came to pass" is like saying you're finally over the hump.

Your fight with fear, your position battle, the issues you've had with self-doubt: they came, but they came to pass. And now they're gone.

If you're an athlete, an artist, or a coach, embracing both meanings of "it came to pass" is of value to you. Having commitments, acting decisively, and expecting greatness are all enhanced with an understanding of "and it came to pass."

What has come to pass in your life this season?
How can you better respect the uniqueness of this season?
What more can you do to honor its value?

What do you need to let go of?
What came, but came to pass, and is now gone?

No Matter What...

Some things come to pass. Make the most of this season. You'll never have another quite like it. Other things come to pass. If you're in a struggle, keep fighting. Know that if you do, in time, this struggle will pass.

ADVERSITY

PART SEVEN

No Conflict = No Story

Fools show their annoyance at once,
but the prudent overlook an insult.
Proverbs 12:16

If you think adventure is dangerous,
try routine. It is lethal.
Paulo Coelho

IMAGINE A WORLD where Anakin Skywalker never becomes Darth Vader. Or a world in which Bruce Wayne is just a guy and Gotham City is an upstanding urban environment. Imagine if Walter White never gets cancer and only teaches chemistry. Or a world where Rocky isn't an underdog and he easily wins every fight he steps into the ring to fight. Difficult to imagine, right?

That's because every good story requires conflict.
The greatest stories have epic conflict.

Unless the circumstances are overwhelming and the odds are stacked against you, we don't pay much attention.

We turn the channel. We close the book. We fall asleep.

In real life, though, conflict is something most of us avoid. I know I do. I prefer to know the costs up front—the less mystery, the better. If there's a more direct, easier route, tell me now because that's the path I'll take. I don't want interruptions. I want to get it right the first time. And the less I have to suffer, the better.

But you know what I just described? A boring story.

Adventure, romance, comedy, thriller: they all require conflict and uncertainty to be any good. A dose of danger here, a pinch of mystery there, and you've got yourself a recipe for something interesting. Why should life be any different?

If you're in a position where you feel like the odds are stacked against you, lean in. Embrace the moment. That giant challenge in front of you is the most interesting part of your story.

If you don't know what's next and the uncertainty is driving you to a breaking point, let it. These are the days you'll tell your grandkids about. Conflict isn't always fun, but it's necessary for a good story. And every athlete, coach, artist, and really, every human being I've ever met, wants to live a good story.

What is the conflict in your life right now?
How do you feel about it?
What are you doing about it?
How can you better embrace the conflict today?

No Matter What...

No conflict = No story. Lean in. Trust God. Live a great story.

No Uncertainty = No Adventure

In all your ways submit to him,
and he will make your paths straight.
Proverbs 3:6

Hope is the power of being cheerful
in circumstances that we know
to be desperate.
GK Chesterton

THE GREATER THE uncertainty, the greater the possible adventure.

The 2014 California Golden Bear football team finished its season with a 5-7 record. Six of those games were decided by seven points or less, three being wins, the other three losses. Two games were decided by only one point, and one game went to double overtime. Of the twelve games on the schedule that season, four were decided on the last play of the game.

Nobody wants to be 5-7; you want to win every game. But, the 2014 season will go down as *the* most exciting season of football I've ever been a part of.

There wasn't a game we played in I didn't think we'd win. No matter the score, I never thought we were out of it. The more uncertain the outcome of a game, the more invested I became. In the same way that a story without conflict is uninteresting, a season without drama is forgettable. No Uncertainty = No Adventure. A journey without uncertainty is just a commute.

Close calls
Overwhelming odds
Nail-biting moments
Disappointment
Triumph
Mystery
Adventure

So many players over the years have come to me frustrated that they don't know what's going to happen next in their careers. Whether it's about their playing time or an injury or the shifting realities of life after football, some guys get quite upset that the future is so unknown. My response to them is always the same: that's what makes this an adventure. Without mystery, you aren't trusting God.

The Scriptures encourage us to live by faith, not by sight. They invite us to trust God no matter what and believe that God can see better than we can. And, trusting God means not knowing. Faith and mystery go hand in hand.

Is there anything you can't see or don't know that keeps you from moving forward? Name it. Say it out loud to a teammate or friend. I find that by saying these kinds of things out loud, we diffuse their power. They don't always go away, but they're not as strong. After you've done that, lean in. Keep moving forward. The 2014 Cal football team didn't win every game, but it kept fighting. No matter the uncertainty, it kept moving forward. What an adventure!

What mystery is present in your life right now?
How is your faith being challenged because of things you don't know?

No Matter What...

No Uncertainty = No Adventure. Enjoy the mystery. Embrace the adventure.

Failure Isn't Final

Better a patient person than a
warrior, one with self-control than
one who takes a city.
Proverbs 16:32

Failure is success in progress.
Alfred North Whitehead

BEFORE HIS FIVE National Championships, Mike Krzyze-wski was nine games under .500 his first three seasons at Duke, going just 38-47 from 1980-1983.

Before his 187 career wins, and having a stadium and a highway named after him, Bill Snyder went 1-10 in 1989, his first year at Kansas State.

Before going 13-3 and winning Super Bowl 34, Dick Vermeil went 4-12 a season earlier as head coach of the St. Louis Rams in 1998.

Failure isn't final. Usually, it's a necessary leg on the journey of success.

Every successful person fails. In athletics, in business, in relationships, in life—no one is immune from the reality of defeat. In fact, those the world sees as most successful have often weathered the most failures. In the words of Michael Jordan, "I've missed more than 9,000 shots in my career. I've lost almost 300 games. Twenty-six times, I've been trusted to take the game-winning shot and missed. I've failed over and over and over again in my life. And that is why I succeed."

One of the most counterintuitive teachings of Scripture is the idea of death and resurrection. That somehow, by dying, we gain life. By struggling, we grow. The winter leaves have to die for spring to come and bloom. An un-pruned plant won't grow to realize its full potential. The same is true of you and me.

Julian of Norwich said, "First the fall, and then the recovery from the fall. And both are the mercy of God." Both the fall and the recovery from the fall are the mercy of God? It makes sense that the recovery from the fall would be the mercy of God, but the fall itself was God's mercy, too? Surely, only those who've weathered the storm, who understood their failure isn't final, know this to be true.

A failure doesn't define you, but it is defining.

Your response to it could be the beginning of something new, a necessary character trait only born in the wake of loss, unmet expectations, or outright defeat. You'll never learn courage without fear, patience without delay, or wisdom without obstacle. Why, then, do you expect to achieve greatness without having to fail along the way?

Where have you failed recently?
What did you learn?
How is God growing you because of it?

One thing is sure; the only way to avoid failure is to never try. And those who hide have failed already.

No Matter What...

Failure isn't final. It's just passing through. Get back up. Breathe. Go again. We need you.

Failure Is Our Great Teacher

When the storm has swept by,
the wicked are gone, but the righteous
stand firm forever.
Proverbs 10:25

If it doesn't challenge you,
it won't change you.
Fred Devito

THE MOMENT OF failure, you have a decision. You either let it define you or you let it inform you.

Carol Dweck, a psychologist whose life's work is the study of success and failure, talks about this decision. In her book, *Mindset*, Dweck argues there are two kinds of mental attitudes in the world: the fixed mindset and the growth mindset. The fixed mindset is only concerned with the appearance of success or intelligence. The growth mindset, on the other hand, is interested in actually learning, regardless of appearance. The implications of this distinction are huge.[23]

The fixed mindset avoids challenges because a failure would give the appearance of weakness or unintelligence. The growth mindset embraces challenges, for there is no other way to learn and grow.

The fixed mindset gives up easily, again, because of how it might look to lose and fall short of a desired outcome. The growth mindset is persistent in the face of setbacks, because obstacles are a chance to gain understanding.

The fixed mindset sees effort as a waste of time. The growth mindset sees effort as the path to mastery.

The fixed mindset avoids criticism and finds negative feedback unuseful. The growth mindset welcomes criticism and learns from what others have to say.

The fixed mindset feels threatened by the success of other people. The growth mindset is inspired by the success of others; there's a lot to learn when others succeed.

Failure isn't final; it's feedback. It is your great teacher.

So you got beat? Okay. What can you learn from it?
You're not getting any playing time? Why?
How can you improve today to give yourself a better chance tomorrow?

No Matter What...

If you learn from them, your failures are never final. Stay curious when things don't go your way. Receive the good with the bad, and get better.

Obstacles Are Opportunities

Whoever loves discipline loves knowledge,
but whoever hates correction is stupid.
Proverbs 12:1

When written in Chinese, the word
crisis is composed of two characters. One
represents danger, and the other represents
opportunity.
John F. Kennedy

OBSTACLES AREN'T ALWAYS what they seem.

In his book *David and Goliath*, Malcolm Gladwell argues that certain disadvantages actually work for the good of those who experience them. He highlights the prevalence of dyslexia in successful entrepreneurs as an example. When interviewed, these entrepreneurs talk about their dyslexia serving them rather than holding them back. Gladwell calls this a desirable disability.

Gladwell also writes about the connection between the death of a parent early in life and the achievement of success later in life. Apparently, for some, great loss encourages a life of striving. He notes that 67 percent of British prime ministers from 1800 to the 1940s lost a parent before the age of 16. He also mentions that a third of the US Presidents, twelve in all, lost their fathers while they were young.[24]

Just because something's easy doesn't mean it's to be desired. In fact, in sports, the opposite is often what you want.

You lift heavier weight in order to get stronger. You compete against more talented opponents so you can sharpen your skills. You run longer distances to increase your endurance.

In sports, obstacles aren't merely a part of the recipe; they're a main ingredient.

The Scriptures talk about God using everything in our lives to make us more whole. Paul writes in the New Testament that God works "in all things for the good of those who love Him." In all things, good things and bad things alike.

What obstacles are you facing?
How are they opportunities?
What can you learn from these obstacles?
How will you respond today?

No Matter What...

Obstacles are opportunities. Welcome them, learn from them, and get better.

"Shit Makes Great Fertilizer"

Whoever spares the rod hates their children,
but the one who loves their children is
careful to discipline them.
Proverbs 13:24

Behind every beautiful thing,
there's some kind of pain.
Bob Dylan

A FEW WEEKS ago, I struck up a conversation with a friend, and he said something that was both funny and true. He was working in his yard shoveling manure into a garden when I arrived, and I immediately took notice of the smell.

"Brandon," I said, "this stinks."

Brandon said, "Sorry, shit makes great fertilizer." I nodded, and we started talking about another friend who'd been going through a rough time. This person recently made some destructive choices in his life, and the consequences were big. I mentioned that I wished our friend's family didn't have to go through it all.

That's when Brandon, while shoveling the last of the manure into the garden, paused, looked up at me and said again, "Yeah, but shit makes great fertilizer."

In that moment, we laughed at what he said, but when I walked away, his comment stayed with me. Manure does make great fertilizer, both in gardening and in life.

Some experiences we go through, we wouldn't want to go through again. At the same time, after having gone through them, we wouldn't trade them for anything in the world.

At 12 years old, Jason Lester was struck by a car and lost all use of his right arm. Forever paralyzed in that arm, no one expected Jason to become the world-class endurance sports athlete he became. He credits his skills as an Ironman and Ultraman endurance champion, in part, to his disability. Having lost the use of his arm at a young age, Jason learned how to endure. He says, "If you don't stop, you can't be stopped."

A breakup. A job loss. The worst season of your life. You don't wish these things upon yourself. But their value could be worth more than a hundred other seasons of things going well.

What tough things are you having to go through right now?
What makes them challenging?
How are you growing because of it all?
How can you continue to grow and learn?

Shit makes great fertilizer. That's if you use it properly. Otherwise, it's just shit.

No Matter What...

The challenges we face in life help us grow. They may stink, but they're full of things we need that we wouldn't get any other way.

The Worst Day = The First Day

A rebuke impresses a discerning person
more than a hundred lashes a fool.
Proverbs 17:10

To say that God turns away from
the sinful is like saying the sun hides
from the blind.
St Anthony the Great

AS A PASTOR, people often confide in me about their
shortcomings. I'm not Catholic, but you could say I regularly
hear confession. This takes on all shapes and sizes.

Some people share with me their judgments of others. Unfor-
giveness, pride, jealousy—fear can look like a lot of different
things. Other people share with me what the church calls sins
of omission, things they feel they should've done but didn't:
taking a risk, reaching out to a friend, or trusting God with
one thing or another. The most difficult conversations—not
for me, for the confessor—are the ones where major sins are
brought out into the open, things like marital unfaithfulness,
substance or alcohol abuse and addiction, or any number of
other hidden, yet destructive patterns of living.

Regardless of the confession, there is a consistency to every conversation. People don't want whatever they're sharing to be known. More often than not, they feel that sharing that thing, whatever it is, will be the worst day of their life. What they don't know yet, though, is that the worst day of their life is often the first day of their testimony. Once they walk through their worst day, a new day awaits them.

I don't know what the worst day of your life is. Maybe you know. Perhaps it hasn't happened yet. In any case, there can only be one worst day. By definition, it's the bottom. It's the lowest you'll go. And by definition, the only direction to go next is up.

Walk through your worst day, and a new day awaits you.

What are you reluctant to bring out into the open?
Why are you so afraid?
What if you can't get to the new day without going through the worst day?

Don't be afraid of the worst day of your life. Receive it. Keep moving and don't stay there. Begin living the first few days of the rest of the story.

No Matter What...

The worst day of life only happens once. Live it out. Go to bed. Wake up a to a new day.

Turn the Page

Give careful thought to the paths for your feet
And be steadfast in all your ways.
Proverbs 4:26

Sometimes you have to forget what's gone,
appreciate what remains, and look
forward to what's coming next.
Unknown

LOSING IS AN event, not a character trait. Go win the next game.

Once all the game film has been watched, once you've learned everything you can from the mistakes you made and the assignments you missed, quit watching. Stop the tape. Go prepare for the next game.

> *Obstacles are opportunities, yes, but once you overcome them, move on. Shit does make great fertilizer, but it also stinks; don't stand in it too long.*

Vytautas (Vitas) Gerulaitis was a Lithuanian American tennis star of the 1970s and 1980s. He won a handful of tournaments in his career, including one major, the 1977 Australian Open. Vitas is probably best remembered for his quick hands and his inability to beat Jimmy Connors. That's because after failing to beat the tennis legend in 16 consecutive tries, Vitas finally won a match against Connors at the January 1980 Masters.

After the win, Vitas said of his victory, "And let that be a lesson to you all. Nobody beats Vitas Gerulaitis 17 times in a row."

I love that. At some point, you just turn the page. You stop allowing the past to define you, and you live a new day.

The psalmist says, "As far as the East is from the West, so has God removed our transgressions from us." God doesn't see us for who we were. He doesn't define us by our missteps and shortcomings. He also doesn't love us for our good deeds and noble accomplishments. God does involve Himself in our missteps and shortcomings. But, God makes them right. He uses them for good. And the whole time, God chooses to love us and make us whole in spite of everything. Remember, this is the truest thing about you.

I don't want to get too far off point, but God isn't Santa Claus. The Scriptures say He keeps no record of wrongs. God doesn't have a nice or a naughty list He's "checking twice." God doesn't give toys to the good little boys and good little girls and coals to everyone else. God loves us all, no matter what. The tit-for-tat kind of god many of us have in our heads isn't the God of the Scriptures.

We do good, God rejoices.
We mess up, God's there to pick us up again.
God's ready to turn the page, to start a new day.

Where do you need to turn the page?
What missteps do you keep focusing on that need to be let go of?

No Matter What...

Once you lose the game, learn from it. Watch the tape, correct your mistakes, then turn the page. Today is a new day.

The Most Dangerous Person

Whoever heeds discipline shows the
way to life, but whoever ignores correction
leads others astray.
Proverbs 10:17

The only character flaws that can really
destroy us are the ones we don't admit.
Tim Keller

THE MOST DANGEROUS person on any team is the one who refuses feedback.

He thinks he's arrived already. She believes she doesn't need coaching. Ignoring flaws, scorning chances to improve, this player is as toxic as it gets.

Get rid of him.
Quickly.

Maybe this person is you, not in totality, but in part. If so, wake up. Snap out of it. Resist every urge to talk yourself out of coaching. Instead, listen. Receive instruction. Yes, God loves you just as you are. But God also invites you to bear fruit. And nobody bears fruit on his or her own.

We all make mistakes. We all need correction. And making mistakes is better than faking perfections. So, work hard, fail forward, and listen to the people around you.

Are you open to correction?
Are you honest about where you've failed?
What have people been trying to tell you that you haven't been able to hear?

No Matter What...

We all have flaws. We all need coaching. Listen. Learn. Grow.

Never Put a Period Where God Puts a Comma

Blessed is the man who remains steadfast
under trial, for when he has stood the test he will
receive the crown of life, which God has promised
to those who love him.
James 1:12

You can't have a better tomorrow
if you're always thinking about yesterday.
Mike Krzyzewski

TWO TEAMS COMPETE; only one wins. There's no guarantee you'll stay healthy, no promise you'll be a star. And the truth is, you most likely won't earn a paycheck pursuing this craft.

Still, win or lose, star or not, God has a plan your life.

God cares about every player, on both sidelines, regardless of what the depth chart says. God's interest in your life isn't tied to your talent, your effectiveness in using that talent, or how long you're able to pursue this dream.

My first season as chaplain, I met a placekicker named David. As a true freshman, David started the first five games of the season, making all 26 of his extra-point attempts and 5 of 7 field goals. He used to tell me stories about those first five games. Before and after practice, the head coach would introduce him to alumni and boosters as "the future career points leader" at Cal.

David was living the dream. True freshman. Starter. Big leg. Big future. He went to bed at night with dreams of the NFL. The sky was the limit. That was before David injured himself just six games into that season. After the injury, his leg was never the same. He didn't play in any game the rest of that first year, and he played in just three games the following season. Redshirting the year after that, David decided to retire from football and graduate from Cal early.

To say this was all pretty tough on David would be an understatement. It was rough, for a while anyway. That's just how it went. And unfortunately, that's how it goes for a lot of guys. Expectations go unmet. Things don't work out as you'd like.

But you move on.
David did.

After losing his starting role and working through the disillusionment that followed, David decided to focus his energy on three things: academics, faith, and dating his future wife, Kendall. He graduated from Cal with a degree, a strong relationship with God, and a beautiful fiancée in tow. Today, David and Kendall live in Washington, DC where he works in politics and she in healthcare. David loves his life and wouldn't trade it for anything in the world.

Here's the thing: David's career at Cal didn't go as planned, but it went exactly how it was supposed to go for him to end up where he is today. David refused to allow his injury and the end of his football career damper his time at Cal. He embraced what God was doing in his life, and today, David's better for it.

I heard a preacher once say, "Never put a period where God puts a comma." Now, that'll preach!

If things haven't turned out how you thought they would, don't shut the book. Just turn the page. God's not done with you yet. Your present circumstances may not look like you thought they would, but that doesn't mean your past was a waste or your future is all lost.

You're going to fall short sometimes. You're going to lose some games. You're going to have expectations go unmet and things not go your way. That's life. But in it all, God continues to work. God doesn't give up. God keeps pursuing. And in all things, God works for the good of those who love Him.

What expectations have gone unmet in your life?
Where have you fallen short?
What is God doing in your life because of it?
How is God working for your good today?

No Matter What...

Never put a period where God puts a comma. Trust God.
Lean in. Keep expecting greatness.

BOUNDARIES

PART EIGHT

You Need Boundaries

I run in the path of your commands,
for you have broadened my understanding.
Psalm 119:32

Boundaries define us. They define what is me
and what is not me. A boundary shows me
where I end and someone else begins,
leading me to a sense of ownership.
Henry Cloud

A CLEAR BOUNDARY doesn't cage you in; it sets you free.

When I was a kid, I used to watch my neighbors' house when they went on vacation. The job was simple enough: I was in charge of getting the mail, walking the dog, and watering all the plants in the yard. Eventually, it was an easy job. I'd drop by once in the morning and again in the evening for about a half hour. Thirty minutes was all it took to finish everything, and I enjoyed the work. It made me feel responsible, grown up. It also didn't hurt that it paid $150 a week, a small fortune for a kid my age at the time.

I say it was "eventually" an easy job, because the first time my neighbors asked me to do it, they neglected to give me clear boundaries. Before they left, they showed me where the dog food was and they showed me all the plants that needed watering, but they forgot to tell me how much food and water to give and how often. Was I supposed to give the dog one scoop of dog food or two, and at every meal? Do dogs even have mealtimes like humans do? And watering the plants, was I supposed to do it every day or every other? All this happened before cell phones, so I didn't have a way to contact my neighbors. They were supposed to call me, and they didn't call for three days.

I was lost. My family never owned a dog, and I was never in charge of watering our plants, so I guessed at everything. Not knowing exactly what I was supposed to do was stressful and frustrating. I ended up overwatering the plants that first week and not feeding the dog near enough. Not having clear boundaries, even with a simple job like this one, left me timid, with unforced errors, and I ended up hurting everything I was responsible to do.

Now, this is a silly story, but the truth within it is something every athlete and coach needs to hear. Boundaries matter. We all need them. Time and energy are limited resources, and if we don't set clear boundaries for both, we'll never steward either well.

People without clear boundaries never have the energy to do the things they want to do in life. People with clear boundaries pursue and complete nearly every project they begin.

People without clear boundaries find themselves doing work emails on date night. People with clear boundaries only do work during work hours.

People without clear boundaries allow toxic, critical people to shape their identity. People with clear boundaries don't allow toxic relationships anywhere near their lives.

The beautiful thing is that when you do have clear boundaries, you're free to just do the work before you. You won't find yourself running out of time, pursuing the wrong relationships, or not having enough energy when you need it. Boundaries aren't a bad thing. They give you clarity. They make you free. Boundaries help you steward your time and energy with wisdom.

Do you have clear, set boundaries for your life?
Can you distinguish between what's your responsibility and what's not your responsibility?
Do you manage your time and energy appropriately?

No Matter What...

You need boundaries. Remember your vision, set goals and make a plan, and be diligent to stay within the boundaries you set for yourself.

Your Tank Is Your Responsibility

If you care for your orchard, you'll enjoy its fruit.
Proverbs 27:18

Half an hour's meditation is essential each day,
except when you are busy. Then a full hour is needed.
Francis De Sales

NOBODY IS RESPONSIBLE for you but you.

A few weeks ago, I ran out of gas. I was running late to a meeting, and when I got in my car, I realized the tank was nearly empty. Thinking I didn't have enough time to stop and fill up, I just went for it.

I didn't make it.

On the side of the road, frustrated, I remember thinking, *What idiot left the tank empty in the first place?* Before I could finish my thought, I remembered who drove the car last: me. I was that idiot.

It's nobody's responsibility but your own to take care of you.

In the same way that it was my responsibility to fill up my car with gas, it's your responsibility to make sure you're energized, enthusiastic, and ready to go each and every day.

I recently spoke with a friend who just graduated. He'd had a distinguished career in college, and his future looks promising in the NFL. When we talked, I asked him what's one thing he thought every incoming freshman should know before they begin their new life as a student-athlete at the highest level? His advice was as practical as it gets.

He said, "Get really good at time management."

Class. Workouts. Relationships. Energy. Rest. These are your responsibility. You have the power to decide where your time will go and what your energy will be given to.

How full is your tank?
How detailed is your schedule?
Are you waiting for someone else to tell you what to do and where to go?

No Matter What...

If you're feeling burned out, don't blame anyone but yourself. Take responsibility. Do what needs to be done to stay focused and engaged.

Invest

If you love sleep, you will end in poverty.
Keep your eyes open, and there will be plenty to eat!
Proverbs 20:13

Days are a finite resource.
It's best to protect the ones you have.
Catherine Lacey

TIME AND ENERGY are limited resources. You only have so much, and every day, at some level, you run out of both.

So what will you do with these limited resources?
Will you invest your time and energy today or will you spend them?

An investment, by definition, expects a return, a future reward on the work you put in. But, an expense? When you merely spend your time and energy on things, you never see them again. There is no return for you to enjoy somewhere down the road.

Investing > spending.

If you could've somehow purchased one share of Coca-Cola

stock in 1919 and simply held on to that one share, reinvesting the dividends along the way, that original $40 investment would be worth over $9.8 million today. If somehow your great, great, great-grandparents could have purchased one share of the original Asa Candlers Coca-Cola stock in 1892, that $100 investment would be worth $7.34 billion today. Translation: it pays to invest your resources and not just spend them.

You spend time and energy when you sleep in, watch television, stream a movie, check social media, or decide to just lay around the house.

You invest time and energy when you study, you work out, you practice, you serve, and you allow yourself to be coached.

Are you doing a good job of stewarding your time and energy?
How can you better invest your time and energy today?
What boundaries can you set to help you?

No Matter What...

You do one of two things with your time and energy: you either invest or you spend. There's no middle ground.

Rest Renews

Without fuel, the fire goes out.
Proverbs 26:20

If I had eight hours to chop down a tree,
I'd spend six sharpening my axe.
Abraham Lincoln

THE SCRIPTURES SAY the people of Israel were enslaved in Egypt for 430 years. That's twelve generations of knowing nothing but work—all day, every day, for a lifetime.

To give you a better picture of what this meant: if the sun was in the sky, the people were at work. The Israelites didn't work from 9-5; they worked from sunup to sundown. They didn't get weekends off. There were no paid vacations. They were slaves. All they knew was slavery and work.

It makes sense, then, that once they were free, God gave Moses the Ten Commandments to help the people better understand how to live life not as slaves. The Ten Commandments were, in part, God's way of directing the people to stop being defined only by work. No longer under Egyptian rule, they needed guidance as to how to treat one another, how to live among one another, and what God might want for them along the way.

The fourth commandment, in particular, invited the people to remember the Sabbath, and to keep it holy. Sabbath, or shabbat, literally means ceasing or stopping. The fourth commandment explicitly called the people to stop being defined by their work. God asked them instead to take one day a week and seek renewal.

Living in the twenty-first century, I've never knowingly met an actual slave. That said, I have met a lot of people who need more of the 4th commandment in their lives. Although most of us didn't grow up twelve generations deep into a work-defined lifestyle, most of us know of no other way of life. We're just as enslaved to our work today as the Israelites were in Moses' day.

Work is a good thing, but it doesn't define you.

Yes, if you want to get where God invites you to go, work is necessary, but so is rest. A car needs refueling to get from here to there. Your body needs food and water every day to survive. The same is true of your creative self; you need refueling. You need to quit work from time to time and seek renewal.

When was the last time you really took a break from your work?
What do you do to get rest?
How can you spend a little time today and be renewed?

If you don't learn how to stop working and rest, you're going to burn out.

No Matter What...

Rest renews. Go get some. Stop being defined only by work, and go refuel.

Strategic Recovery

Whatever you do, do well.
Ecclesiastes 9:10

Anyone can see the adversity in a difficult situation,
but it takes a stronger person to see the opportunity.
Drew Brees

WHAT SEPARATES GREAT competitors from poor ones?

In the mid 1980s, Dr. Jim Loehr, co-founder of the Human Performance Institute, studied the top 50 tennis players in the world, hoping to discover what separated a great tennis player from an average one. At first, his research focused on the "during point time" of a tennis match, the time when the players are actually hitting the ball back and forth. But, looking at this data alone, he saw no distinctions.

Dr. Loehr says, "There was nothing there. All of them had great biomechanics, had great movement. It was very difficult to determine who were the great competitors, who were the ones who could actually pull their best out at the critical moments, just looking at that 'during point time.'"

What's crazy about tennis, though, is that only 35 percent of a match is actually spent hitting a ball. The other 65 percent of the time is spent outside of "during point time," when a player is just regrouping and getting ready to serve or receive serve. Known as "dead time," an average 16-second break occurs between every point. Dr. Loehr and his team refocused their study to examine these 16-second moments, or 65 percent of a match. What they discovered is fascinating.

Great players maximize their "dead time." Average players do not. "During point time" in any sport is stressful. It requires the body to work, and it drains the mind of energy. Dr. Loehr and his team noticed that great players understand this, and they use dead time to recover from the stress by regaining energy. In what is known as "strategic recovery," the great tennis players used their dead time to do at least four things: imagine a positive physical response, relax, mentally prepare, and go through a ritual.

Imagine a positive physical response. This is where a player replays the previous point in her head and imagines the correction that needed to occur. Instead of fixating on the error, the player replaces that image with the correct movement or shot.

Relax. After replacing the image, the player relaxes by taking a few deep breaths.

Mentally prepare. The player looks into the court and imagines the next shot. She sees the next serve, visualizes the next swing, and plays the point out in her head.

Go through a ritual.

Finally, before the player hits the ball, she goes through a few rituals. This is where the player bounces the tennis ball a few times, lifts her head twice, or touches her shoulder just before serving.

Great players took advantage of every break offered them. By practicing the steps of strategic recovery, they regained the energy needed to play the next point. Average and poor players, on the other hand, did nothing meaningful with their dead time. They often rolled their eyes, wallowed in their failure, and visibly displayed their frustration. They didn't see dead time"as an opportunity for recovery, and that's what kept them from being great.

What does all this mean? Getting good at time management is only half the battle. Understanding and stewarding your energy well, seeing dead time as an opportunity for recovery, is what wins the war.

Do you recover well?
In the moments you're not performing, what are you thinking about?
What is your focus?
Are you able to refocus after a tough play?
How can you get better at this?

Ecclesiastes 9:10 says, "Whatever you do, do well." This includes "during point time and "dead time." Do well in whatever you do.

_____

No Matter What...

Time management is important, but energy management is
what propels you to realize your full potential.

Move Fast; Live Slow

Be still, and know that I am God.
Psalm 46:10

Hurry is a form of violence practiced on time.
Time is sacred.
Eugene Peterson

JESUS ONCE ASKED, "What good is it to gain the whole world and forfeit your soul? Is anything worth more than your soul?"

We live in a world where athletes and coaches regularly trade their integrity for even the slightest advantage over an opponent. And for what?

A trophy?
Some money?
Fifteen minutes of fame?

Perhaps the most famous cheater of the last two decades is Lance Armstrong, the 7-time Tour de France winner who battled back from cancer to become a national hero and himself an international brand bigger than the sport. His legacy was forever damaged when he finally confessed to having doped throughout his career.

Many have demonized Armstrong for his defiant deceit. For years, he fabricated stories of being clean, proclaiming he was the victim of jealous rivals who were bitter they couldn't keep up. What we all didn't know, though, was that his lie was bigger than himself. The entire sport of cycling followed the omertà, or code of silence, denying the endemic of doping that had become the sport.

How does this happen?
How does one man become so committed to such an egregious lie?
How does an entire sport forfeit its soul to become a faction of cheaters?

Well, it doesn't happen overnight.

No one trades in their soul all at once. It happens little by little. A small compromise here. A "harmless" bending of the rules there. You don't see it coming, but before long, small lies create a burden of deceit. Unintentionally, you become dependent on the compromise. And with time, you're forced into covering it up. No one sets out to become "the most famous cheater of the last two decades." What happens is that a single lie becomes a web of lies, and before long, you get caught up in it. That's what happened to Lance. That's what happened to cycling. Is it happening to you?

The only antidote I know to getting caught up in something is to, with regularity, slow down and see.

Are you moving too fast?
In a hurried pace of life, are you tempted to cut corners or compromise the truth?
Have you gotten caught up in something you know isn't good for you?

Psalm 46:10 says, "Be still, and know that I am God." This psalm is an invitation to stop being in such a hurry, to slow down, and remember God. It's an invitation to be honest about the work you've done, the person you're becoming, and have the courage to change course if you don't like what you see.

You can only do this if you slow down.
If you're in a hurry, you won't stop.
You won't take the time to see.
You won't be honest.

And this lie is the greatest of all lies—the one we tell ourselves—that everything is okay when it isn't, that we're doing just fine when we really aren't. It's okay to move fast. Realizing your goals probably requires that you do. But learn to live slowly. Learn to take time for honest reflection. Don't allow yourself to compromise your values for anything.

No Matter What...

There is never a good reason to forfeit your soul. Be honest. Stay true to your values. If you're going to do this, you'll need to learn the art of living slowly.

Celebrate the Right Things

Where your treasure is,
there your heart will be also.
Matthew 6:21

Understanding what not to do is sometimes
just as important as what you can do.
Bill Belichick

WHAT STORYLINE DO you care about most?

In grad school, I had a professor who argued that artists—songwriters, filmmakers, and sports icons—were more influential in shaping culture than every other segment of society combined. He believed that these culture-creators were first and foremost storytellers. He'd often say, "The stories they celebrate shape the culture we all live in."

In collegiate athletics, there are plenty of stories to celebrate.

The Individual Storyline: Going Pro.
For the player, this storyline is about making it to the NFL or the NBA or the Olympics. For the coach, it's about moving up, from position coach to coordinator to head coach and, potentially, one day jumping to a different league. This storyline

provokes big dreams; however, it struggles to remain present in the opportunities and blessings of today.

The Winner Storyline: Win at All Costs.

This storyline cares most about one thing: winning—at all costs, every game, no matter what. For some, winning is the only reason to play the game. Without it, none of this means anything. The winner storyline encourages competition, toughness, and focus. It can also produce distracting ways of thinking, like comparison, fear, and being shortsighted.

The Mindset Storyline: Just Get Better.

For many, improving is the focus. Winning and potentially going pro are secondary to, and only accomplished if, getting better is the goal. Here, sports aren't only about winning and losing; sports are about character transformation. Sports are about becoming better human beings.

The Family Storyline: It's All About the Team.

For these athletes, life is about relationship. What better environment to make memories, to be a friend, and to compete than on a team at this level?

The Student-Athlete Storyline: I'm Here to Get an Education.

For some student-athletes, student > athlete. At Cal, these players understand choosing UC Berkeley was a 40-year decision, not a 4-year decision. In terms of coaching, an education storyline turns the coach into mentor, not just for the sport, but for all of life.

What storyline do you care about the most?
Going pro, winning, getting better, the team, getting an education, or something else?
What storyline is most important to God?

What story you choose goes a long way in deciding where you'll end up.

No Matter What...

The stories you celebrate shape you. Celebrate the right things, and this whole experience could be great.

How You Do Anything Is How You Do Everything

Whoever walks in integrity walks securely,
but whoever takes crooked paths will be found out.
Proverbs 10:9

Everything is practice.
Pelé

EVERYTHING MATTERS.

Each season on the first day of practice, John Wooden famously called a team meeting for a single purpose: to show his players how to properly put on their shoes and socks. Wooden believed that if a player learned to lace up his shoes correctly, he was learning, "…everything he'd need to know for the rest of his life."

Coach Wooden said, "Basketball is a game that's played on a hardwood floor. And to be good you have to change your direction, change your pace. That's hard on your feet. And if you don't have every wrinkle out of your sock…the wrinkle will be sure to get you blisters, and those blisters are going to make you lose playing time, and if you're good enough, your loss of playing time might get the coach fired."

There's a term in psychiatry called synchronicity. Synchronicity is defined as the simultaneous occurrence of events that appear significantly related but have no discernible causal connection. In other words, synchronicity is when your brain connects two seemingly unconnected things.

What is synchronicity?

Synchronicity means that lacing up your shoes properly is directly connected to your playing time and your coach's job security.

Coach Mark Tommerdahl likes to tell the story of a player he coached who was under-realizing his full athletic potential— until one day this player went from being a backup running back to an all-conference performer. When Coach asked the player how he'd refocused his game, the player responded, "That's easy. I started making my bed." For this player, making his bed in the morning—doing even a small thing the proper way—began to show up in other areas of his life.

What is tying your shoes?
What is making your bed?

They're small things, small tasks you accomplish before you ever get out on the field.

Coach Tommerdahl says when he heard the player say, "I started making my bed," it made perfect sense. On the field of play, this player's game had changed in similar ways. He started every practice fully engaged. He finished every play with 100% effort. The small things he used to ignore were now getting his full attention.

How you do anything is how you do everything.

If you're halfhearted in the classroom, you'll be the same on game days. If you pay more attention to your phone than you do to your coach when watching film, you're not going to listen during a game either. If, however, you begin to pay attention to the small things in your life, that'll show up on the field, too. If you finish your assignment on time, you'll finish every workout. If you practice with 100 percent intensity, game time will receive the same effort. From how organized you are in your apartment to how well you treat your roommates, it all shows up on the field.

Do you lace up your shoes properly?
Do you make your bed? Why or why not?
What things can you improve outside of your sport?

No Matter What...

Everything is practice. Stop pretending your life isn't connected when it is. Who you are when no one is looking is who you are when everyone is watching.

The Culture of Your Life

Steep your life in God-reality, God-initiative, God-provisions.
Don't worry about missing out. You'll find all your
everyday human concerns will be met.
Matthew 6:33 (MSG)

Culture beats scheme every time.
Chip Kelly

Culture (*noun*): (1) the customs and attitudes, values and
practices of a particular society, group, or
organization.
(2) a way of life shared by people in a certain
place and time.

APR STANDS FOR Academic Progress Rate. It measures
the likelihood of graduation for student-athletes within a
specific sport. It was widely publicized a few years ago that
Cal Football was among the lowest APR scores of any FBS
program in the country. For a sports program at Cal, otherwise known as UC Berkeley—the top-rated public institution
in the country—this was beyond unacceptable. To receive
such low academic marks, something had to be done.

So, in came a new coaching staff, and with them, a whole bunch of new routines and attitudes. One of the first changes I noticed may have been the most subtle, but in my opinion, it was among the most important.

The entryway to the Cal Football office suite is decorated with large display cases and prominent frames for photos and memorabilia. The purpose, of course, is not just to highlight facts about the program, but to tell a story about what this place is all about.

Now, during the years of the low APR scores, the displays and picture frames showcased former Cal Football players who'd made it to the NFL. Images of top draft picks holding up Super Bowl trophies were huge and impossible to ignore. The story being communicated was obvious: come to Cal, and you'll get drafted; this is a place where NFL stars are born. The problem with this storyline, though, is that it created a "me" culture. I don't believe it was intentional, but it did. Certain players were self-absorbed, entitled, and many didn't care about the classroom at all.

With the new coaching staff came new displays. Out were images of the NFL, and in came huge photos of student-athletes graduating and earning their degree. Pictures of players in the classroom, at work studying, and receiving academic support were everywhere. The new story being told was clear: come to Cal, and you'll get one of the best educations the world has to offer.

Culture matters because environments matter. Some things only happen in very specific environments. You cannot grow Florida oranges in Alaska. You will never walk the Great Wall of China on a visit to South Africa. A person doesn't lose weight eating donuts every day for breakfast and lunch. In the case of Cal, you won't produce high APR scores only celebrating life after college; you must celebrate life in the classroom today.

What about you? What is the culture of your life?
What customs, rituals, attitudes, and practices are influencing you?

From the music you listen to, to the food you eat, to the people you follow on social media, you are creating a culture with every decision you make.

Is the culture of your life healthy?
Is God a part of the culture of your life?

No Matter What...

Your life has a culture, and it's shaping you in more ways than you know. Be intentional with your decision-making. Create a culture that produces the results you're aiming for.

Necessary Endings

For everything there is a season,
a time for every activity under heaven.
Ecclesiastes 3:1

Saying yes to one thing is saying no to something else.
Andy Stanley

SOMETIMES IN LIFE, if you want to go anywhere new, you have to detach yourself from an idea, a routine, and in some cases, a person.

A few years ago, a friend called asking if I'd pray for him. He and his wife were about to buy a house, and he was on his way to the bank to make the down payment. To say he was nervous is an understatement. He had the money. That wasn't the problem. No, what he was worried about was the loss of his life savings. Writing that check meant handing over more than $100,000 of his security and peace of mind. Not only that, in buying the house, he was also indebting himself to the bank for years to come.

We talked on the phone about whether or not he really wanted to own a home. He said he did.

"Then this is one of those moments where you get to tangibly trust God." I said. "Security and peace of mind are two things you must be willing to let go of if you want to experience the new reality of owning your own home."

Psychologist and author Henry Cloud says, "For whatever God has for you to do tomorrow, it requires probably that you stop doing something today."

My friend needed to say goodbye to the idea of peace and security. What do you need to say goodbye to? It could be a habit or a daily ritual that isn't supporting your vision. It could be a person, someone who isn't for you. Critics, naysayers, and opponents have their place, but sometimes it's best to just move on. This could even mean needing to move on from a friend.

The point is, if you're stuck, it's possible nothing new needs to be created. No, perhaps what's keeping you from realizing the future God's inviting you into is your inability to end things. Have the courage to say goodbye.

What do you need to stop doing today?
What habits are holding you back?
Are there any ideas you need to let go of?
Is there a relationship you must walk away from in order to realize your God-given potential?

No Matter What...

Moving forward often means saying goodbye. Necessary endings aren't optional; they're necessary if you want to go anywhere new.

FEAR

PART NINE

Fear, but Don't Be Afraid

The fear of the Lord is the beginning of
all wisdom and discipline.
Proverbs 1:7

Fear only has the power we give it.
Hope works the same way.
Bob Goff

THERE ARE TWO kinds of fear: the fear of man and the
fear of God. At any given moment, you live from one or the
other, and they couldn't be more different.

The fear of man paralyzes you. The fear of God sets you free.
The fear of man is based on judgment. The fear of God is
grace and peace. The fear of man leaves you insecure and ev-
er-doubting. The fear of God gives you enduring strength and
courage.

So, what does it meant to fear God? Unlike the fear of man,
which is based on the threat of danger, pain or terror, the fear
of God is about presence and love and trust.

To fear God is first about presence.
It's recognizing that God is here, present in every moment,

holding all things together. Whether it's a sunrise, a morning run, or the fourth quarter of the big game, there is an inherent dignity in everything you experience—wins and losses, joys and sorrows alike. To fear God is first to recognize this dignity, to nod your head to God's presence in each moment you find yourself within.

Next, the fear of God is about love.
God is perfect love. To fear God is to identify with God's perfect love, to live from that love. This is the best part: when you identify wholly with God's perfect love, the fear of man can't touch you. You're no longer enslaved to what others think. You can finally retire from the tireless work of keeping up appearances. You're loved already, no matter what. You don't have to prove anything to anybody when you remember your true self.

Finally, the fear of God is about trust.
Along with acknowledging God's presence and identifying with God's love, to fear God is to trust God. It's giving up the need to have all the answers, and to step out in faith. When you can only see the next move, it's trusting that God sees the whole board. To fear God is to rely upon this knowledge, to depend on God's provision, and to go for it.

So, what are you afraid of?
Are you afraid of what others think and feel?
Do you live an insecure, fragile existence?
How is God present in this moment, right now?

No Matter What...

There are two kinds of fear the fear of man and the fear of God. You always live your life from one or the other.

Fear Is a Story

Don't be afraid. Just have faith.
Mark 5:36

What if instead of fears, we called them stories?
That's what fear really is, a story that we tell ourselves.
It's a kind of unintentional storytelling that
we all are born knowing how to do.
Karen Thompson Walker

YOUR FEARS ARE just stories.

Author Karen Thompson Walker likens fears to stories, saying, "Fears and stories have the same components. They have the same architecture. Like all stories, fears have characters. In our fears, we are the characters. They have plots; they have beginnings and middles and ends. 'You board the plane, the plane takes off, the engine fails…' We all know what fear feels like, but do we know what our fears mean? What if we looked at fear as a story, as a powerful act of imagination?"[25]

The way most people talk about fear gives it too much power.

You conquer fear. You overcome it.

It's something you fight against. It's something that holds you back.

But if fear is just a story, then you always have a choice to believe whether it's true or not. You have the power to project yourself into that fearful story, or you can decide to project yourself into a different one. It's entirely up to you which story is worth believing.

A friend recently shared with me that he thought his coach didn't like him. He was afraid that no matter what he did, he could never earn his coach's favor. Unfortunately, like all of us, this fear led to all kinds of other fears. Afraid of his coach's opinion, my friend grew timid and judgmental whenever he was in his presence. My friend stopped speaking up in meetings, he refused to ask his coach for help, and eventually, he quit working hard in practice, for fear of being noticed at all. One fear led to another, and on and on.

When we talked, I asked my friend, "But what if your coach does like you? What if you're misinterpreting his coaching style and taking things too personally? Wouldn't that change things?"

It's amazing how believing one false storyline can lead to all kinds of crazy storylines, none of which are close to being true. This is called over-concluding.

Make no mistake, fear is a powerful act of imagination. It's powerful because it can confuse, paralyze, overwhelm, provoke, and intimidate you. But if you remember your fear is just a story, then you're free to choose what's true and what's false.

What are you afraid of?
Is that fear a true story?
What if it's not true? How would you live differently?

Where are you over-concluding?

No Matter What...

Fear is a story you can choose to believe or not believe. It is a powerful act of your imagination.

Faith Is Like Fear

Don't be afraid. Just have faith.
Mark 5:36

It's lack of faith that leads people to be afraid
of meeting challenges, and I believed in myself.
Mohammad Ali

FAITH IS A story, too.

Stories are everywhere. We entertain ourselves with stories. We read them. We watch them. Our experiences are stories. They're how we talk about our days, and they're the medium through which we remember the past. We know what stories are, but do we know what they do?

Every good story does two things; great stories do three things. Good stories evoke emotion and facilitate imagination. Great stories do these, but they also fuel action.

Stories evoke emotion.
Stories, good and great, invite us to feel something. Comedies make us laugh, tragedies make us cry, and thrillers keep us on the edge of our seats. Fear is a story that leads us to feel alone,

helpless, overwhelmed, and timid. But faith? Faith is a story that leads us to feel comforted, powerful, clear-headed, and secure.

Stories facilitate imagination.
Good and great stories invite us to create a world that doesn't exist in reality. We see things that aren't there, project ourselves into scenarios that don't exist, and become people we've never allowed ourselves to be.

Fear imagines a world in which our circumstances harm us. We imagine ourselves the victim of some dire, uncomfortable storyline. Faith, on the other hand, imagines a world where our circumstances don't define us. Faith doesn't merely talk to God about our circumstances. Faith talks to our circumstances about God. Faith allows us to imagine ourselves rising above those circumstances, being defined by something else.

Great stories fuel action.
Great stories compel us to do something. Now, by great, I don't mean good or bad; I just mean a compelling story, one we project ourselves into with ease.

Fear is a story that fuels us in negative ways. Fear can lead us to run. Fear can paralyze us to stay. Fear can provoke us to war. Fear can force us to sign a treaty of peace. Faith, though, is a story that fuels the best in us. Faith fuels us toward love, joy, peace, patience, kindness, goodness, meekness, and self-control. Faith fuels us to risk, to create, to do something we've never done before for the good of those around us.

Mark 5:36 says, "Don't be afraid. Just have faith." For years, when I read this passage, I thought, *Right, Jesus, as if I wasn't trying. If it were that easy, I promise You, I'd do it.* But what I never understood was that like fear, faith is a story we get to choose to believe or not believe. Jesus knew fear and faith were both stories. He understood that they produce the same kinds of things: emotions, imagination, and action. By saying, "just have faith," Jesus is inviting us to exercise the same muscles we would with fear, but in a new, better way.

Do you tell yourself stories of fear or stories of faith?
What fear stories must you replace with faith stories?
Are you merely talking to God about your circumstances?
What would it take for you to talk to your circumstances about God?

No Matter What...

Faith is a story, too. It is a powerful act of your imagination.

Courage > Self

The wicked run away when no one is chasing them,
but the godly are as bold as lions.
Proverbs 28:1

Courage isn't the absence of fear.
Courage is the absence of self.
Erwin McManus

THE MOST COURAGEOUS people in the world also happen to be the most selfless.

Sociologist and author Brene Brown has spent her entire professional life studying courage. After years of research, writing, teaching, and offering her expertise to audiences around the world, she concludes there is really only one accurate way to measure the level of courage in a human being: vulnerability. A person's willingness to be vulnerable, to open him or herself up to injury, failure, and embarrassment, is the only accurate way to see how courageous that person is in real life.[26]

If Dr. Brown is right, if vulnerability is the best way to measure courage, then just one question needs to be asked: how selfish are you?

Selfish people are only concerned with themselves. Their first thought is of their own well-being, their own desires, and themselves coming out on top. By definition, selfish people are the least likely people to be vulnerable—and conversely, by Brene Brown's standard, the least courageous.

Scan a list of history's most courageous people, and it will read like a roll call of selflessness. Galileo Galilei, Frederick Douglass, Dietrich Bonhoeffer, Anne Frank, Rosa Parks, Martin Luther King, Jr., Mahatma Gandhi, not to mention, Jesus of Nazareth. These people were willing to sacrifice their reputation, their well-being, and in some cases, their lives, for what they were committed to creating. They weren't selfish. They believed in something bigger than themselves.

Are you afraid? Is it holding you back?
Have you ever considered that it might be because you're too selfish?

There's a passage in the New Testament of the Bible that says, "Do not merely look out for your own interests, but look out for the interests of others. Consider others more than yourself. In fact, if you've ever gotten anything out of following after God, then do what Jesus did: give your life away for the people around you. Be courageous like He was" (Philippians 2, my translation).

Courageous people aren't without fear. It's just that they're not primarily concerned with their own well-being. They're too busy serving people, committed to a cause, to stay focused on their fear. Courage is their ability to move forward and be vulnerable, despite the fear, for the betterment of everything around them.

Where is God inviting you to be more vulnerable?
How can you step out today, despite your fears?
Who are you doing this for?

No Matter What...

Courage is selfless, not fearless. Take the next step, risk, put yourself out there—not for you, but for the people around you.

Fear Appeal

Oh, the joys of those who do not follow
the advice of the wicked, or stand around
with sinners, or join in with mockers.
Psalm 1:1

The enemy is fear.
We think it is hate, but it is fear.
Gandhi

IT'S IN SOME people's best interest to keep you afraid.

A fear appeal is a persuasive message meant to arouse fear in order to influence decision making. It's basically a marketing strategy designed to prey on your fears. Salesmen use it, so do politicians; and unfortunately, many pastors I know use it, too.

"Your car could break down at any moment with an old engine like this one. Think about your family; do you want to end up broken down on the side of some highway with these beautiful kids? Why not let me give it a full tune-up along with this oil change, just so we're safe?"

"Our country is coming unglued. Terrorists are out to get us.

Your jobs aren't secure. And our kids' futures have never been more in jeopardy. Vote for me, and I'll keep you safe."

"If you died tonight, do you know where you'd go? God offers you heaven, but if you don't pray this prayer, He'll send you to hell. Now, would you like to pray with me?"

Fear appeal is everywhere. It may seem silly when you know what to look for, but, at school, on the field, and in your relationships, it's one of the most dominant ways people aim to manipulate you to their agenda. Keeping you afraid is big business. But it is no way to live.

> *Who in your life is preying on your fears?*
> *How many decisions have you made based on fear in the last two months?*

One of the best places to start taking inventory is your friends.

> *Have you surrounded yourself with people who allow you to live in fear? Or do your friends help you identify fear and work with you to overcome it?*

Psalm 1:1 says, "Do not sit with mockers, or run with sinners, or take the advice of the wicked." This is basically a call to be intentional with those you spend time with. It's all too easy to surround yourself with people who either prey on your fears or who allow you to make decisions based on fear because they themselves are afraid of the same things.

> *Refuse to live your life in fear.*

No Matter What...

Quit making decisions based on fear. Live a courageous life. Surround yourself with people who encourage you to keep having faith, to keep stepping out.

Faith - (___) ≠ Faith

We live by faith, not by sight.
2 Corinthians 5:7

Success in the sport is, above all else,
about enduring suffering.
Chris McCormack

FAITH DOESN'T ALWAYS feel good.

Earlier this year I, along with a group of 20 other leaders, did a training exercise where we explored what faith felt like. The facilitator began the exercise by drawing a large X on a whiteboard. He then drew a circle around the X. He said the X represents us, and the circle represents everything we're capable of on our own—all the knowledge, talent, and experience we carry with us wherever we go. Within the circle lives everything we're capable of doing without having to live by faith.

He then drew another X far outside the circle. He said this X represents the future God invites us into. It could be a project we care about, a relationship we hope to be transformed, or a vision for ourselves we've yet to attain. Next, he drew a line connecting the two Xs. This line, he said, represents the journey of faith God asks us to take.

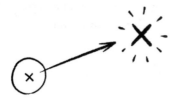

Finally, he asked us, "What does it feel like to travel along this line, from the X inside the circle to the X outside, and become the person God invites us to become? What does it feel like to step out in faith?"

Think about a time when you stepped out in faith. It doesn't matter the context, just imagine what it felt like.

> *What were you thinking?*
> *How comfortable were you doing it?*
> *Did you feel strong or weak, alone or in community?*

Well, the group spent the next half hour telling stories of faith, and as people shared, it became clear that faith often feels really uncomfortable. At times, it's downright awful. Here are examples of what people said faith felt like to them:

Blind. Silly. Unknown. Uncomfortable. Adventure. Risky. Exciting. Vulnerable. Stretching. Change. Dependence. Lonely. Growth. Courageous. Open to persecution. Mysterious. Slowing down. Lack of control. Believing in something. Reliance on others. Obedience. Higher level of accountability. More aware. Guaranteed failure. Rewarding. Scary. Impactful. Frustrating.

Sacrificial. Love. Hope. Glorifying.

Faith doesn't always feel good. But that's what makes it faith. If you take away any of the above feelings or realities, you haven't left the circle. You're not living by faith.

Faith - (_____) ≠ Faith.

Faith without uncertainty is not faith.
Faith without perseverance is not faith.
Faith without doubt is not faith.
Faith without feeling silly at times is not faith.
Faith without the chance of failure is not faith.

Are you living inside the circle or outside?
How do you feel about stepping out in faith?
Have you reminded yourself that this is what it's supposed to feel like to trust God?

No Matter What...

Trusting God isn't always comfortable. If you're frustrated, uncertain, feeling silly, alone, or like you're on an adventure, then you might just be right where God wants you to be.

Fret Not

Do not fret.
Psalm 37:8

Pray as though everything depended on God.
Work as though everything depended on you.
St. Augustine

DO NOT FRET.

Fear has a cousin. She's less talked about, and you don't always know when she's around. But she can be all-consuming, and she threatens your very existence—your confidence, your ability to do anything meaningful with today. Her name is fretting, and you'd do well to examine if she's anywhere near your life.

Fret is defined as a constant or visible worry; anxiety. It's like a low-grade fever of fear. The word *fret* in Hebrew is *haran*, which means to burn, kindle, or to be inflamed. That's appropriate, because that's exactly what fretting does to your soul. Its slowly eats away at your self-worth and faith.

I've heard many athletes over the years talk about nagging injuries. Offensive linemen mention to me that their hands and feet are always hurting. They say they can't do much about it in season, though, because that's just how it goes.

The word *nagging* is the perfect metaphor for understanding what fretting feels like. It's just there, often beneath the surface, nagging you. You don't always pay attention to it, but it's present. And if you took the time to stop and reflect, you'd agree it's tearing you up inside.

Are you fretting?
Is there a below-the-surface fear nagging you today?

Psalm 37 is pretty clear about what we're supposed to do with fretting. "Do not fret," it says. About fretting: do not do it. There is no wiggle room there. Do not allow yourself to fret. Unlike the other nagging injuries you force yourself to endure, fretting isn't something you're supposed to live with.

Psalm 37 goes on to say you should replace your fretting with faith in God. How do you do this? Start by naming it.

The first step to overcoming this kind of fear is to talk about it. If you're fretting, tell someone. Tell a friend what's bothering you, what you're worried about. I find that sharing my anxieties robs them of their sting. Next, Psalm 37 encourages us to replace our worry with action. For example, if you're worried about your health, replace your worry with a plan. Eat better, stretch regularly, and get good sleep every night of the week. If you're worried about playing time or how you'll perform, outline what you can actually accomplish in a day, and every day, do those things. Rest well each night knowing you did what you could to squelch your worry.

Finally, pray. Don't pray so that God will change your circumstances or take away the things you're worried about. No, pray to change your own mind about how you view those circumstances. St. Augustine said, "Pray as though everything depended on God. Work as though everything depended on you."

Do you have a low-grade fever of fear? What's worrying you?
Who will you tell about these anxieties?
What can you do instead of worrying?

Pray and commit your work to the Lord.

No Matter What...

Do not fret. Name your fears, especially the subtle ones. Do the work before you, and commit that work to the Lord.

This Is Why We Pray

In everything, by prayer and petition,
present your requests to the Lord.
Philippians 4:6-7

We pause to listen to the beat of
your Presence in all things.
John Philip Newell

PRAYER IS THE means by which God shapes us, not the
other way around.

Author and theologian Peter Rollins tells a great story about a
little boy experimenting with prayer: "When I was a kid, I used
to pray every night for a new bike," said the little boy. "Then,
I realized God doesn't work like that. So, I just stole one and
asked Him to forgive me."

This story is meant to be funny, and it is.
But it's also all too true.

Most of us approach prayer the same way as this little boy. Our
prayers are negotiations with God. Prayer is how we bargain
with God to get something we want or something we think we
need, all the while hoping God will deliver. Now, there is noth-

ing wrong with asking God for a new bike or to heal our sick grandma or something else, but we must at least acknowledge just how self-centered this kind of praying can be.

There's a guy in the New Testament of the Bible named Paul. He was a towering figure in the establishment of the early church. He was a missionary, a church-planter, and he wrote over half of the New Testament letters and writings. Prayer is a favorite topic of Paul's. He regularly calls his readers to reach out to God in prayer. What's telling, though, is that in all of his recorded prayers and commentary on prayer, Paul never asks God for a change in circumstance. He never asks God to give him a new bike, freedom from persecution or imprisonment (both of which he experienced), and he never asks for material wealth or status or achievement.

No, prayer for Paul was always about changing Paul.

> *The primary purpose of prayer isn't to get God to do anything, but to be properly formed. Prayer isn't how we get things from God, but how we get more of God Himself.*

If you're struggling, you may or may not require more resources, better health, or improved conditions, but you can always benefit from more of God. God's presence, love, and grace always strengthen us when we face fear, anxiety, or worry. This is why we pray: to invite God to change us. Prayer is how we become more aware of God's perspective, God's power, and God's view of the conditions we're up against.

> *Why do you pray?*
> *What do you want?*
> *What if God simply gives you more of His presence and perspective on things? How is that a good thing?*

Sometimes, we don't need new horizons; we just need new eyes. That's what prayer is all about.

_____

No Matter What...

Prayer shapes you more than it shapes God. Pray and be present to God's presence in your life. Ask God for more of His perspective and less of your own.

A Belief > A Circumstance

The wisdom of the prudent is to give thought to their ways,
but the folly of fools is deception.
Proverbs 14:8

Everything can be taken from us but one thing,
to choose one's attitude in any circumstance.
Viktor Frankl

THE ONLY THING more powerful than a circumstance is a belief.

Viktor Frankl was an Austrian psychiatrist, neurologist, and Holocaust survivor. Before his deportation to the Nazi Theresienstadt Ghetto in 1942, Frankl worked as a physician and therapist, offering relief to tens of thousands of women struggling with suicidal tendencies. In 1944, he and his family were taken to the Auschwitz concentration camp, and moved from camp to camp over the next several months under Nazi rule. During that time, Frankl's mother, brother, and wife were all killed by the Nazis.

When the war ended in 1945, Frankl wrote about his experiences in his book *Saying Yes to Life in Spite of Everything: A*

Psychologist Experiences the Concentration Camp, or as it is known in the US, *Man's Search for Meaning.*

In this classic work, Frankl writes, "Everything can be taken from us but one thing, to choose one's attitude in any circumstance."[27]

> *What are you afraid of?*
> *What circumstances are you up against?*
> *Is there anywhere in your life you're tempted to give up, to give in, or to stop trusting God?*

Listen to Viktor Frankl.

It may seem as though everything has been taken from you, but you're always in control of how you feel. No one can take your will to survive. No one can take your choice to choose how you're going to feel toward a given circumstance or obstacle.

> *How do you feel about the obstacles you're facing?*
> *Is there another option? Could you choose to feel differently? If so, how?*
> *Is it possible you've given your circumstances, your fears, and other people too much authority over how you feel and what you believe is true?*

Fear only has the power you allow it. What you believe about a circumstance is always more powerful than the circumstance itself.

No Matter What...

Take control of your thoughts. Refuse to allow circumstances to dictate how you feel. This is what faith is; this is how your belief becomes more than a creed or an idea.

Perfect Love > Fear

There is no fear in love.
Perfect love drives out fear.
1 John 4:8

I've experienced many terrible things in my life,
a few of which actually happened.
Mark Twain

PERFECT LOVE DRIVES out fear.

If you were to take all the commandments of Scripture, total them up by how many times each is given, and stack them next to one another, one commandment would stand tall above the rest:

"Do not fear."

Be not afraid. Don't fret. Take courage. Fear not. Be strong and courageous. In one form or another, "do not fear" is found in the Bible nearly 400 times. If God wants you to know anything, God wants you to know this: you don't have to be afraid anymore.

God didn't create you, give you the talent you possess and the passion that drives you so that today you'd cower in fear. No, God created you to go for it. God wants you to show up, to believe in yourself, and to offer your gifts to the world with courage and faith.

If you're thinking, *Yeah, that sounds good and all, but you don't know what I'm up against.* Or, *But what if I fail? What if I give it my all and nobody wants what I have to offer?*

> *First of all, who are you to say nobody wants what you have to offer? And, what good will you not trying do for anybody?*

You'll never know unless you reach out.

By the way, you shouldn't be worried what the rest of us think. Don't build your life on our opinion of you. Remember your true self in God? That part of you that is completely and unconditionally loved? Start there. Live from that healthy place before you go anywhere or create anything.

First John 4 says, "There is no fear in love. Perfect love drives out all fear." Your true self is that perfect love. If you choose to live from this place, then the fear that is holding you back won't have the power you've given it in the past.

> *What are you still afraid of?*
> *Have you considered what perfect love really means? Do you believe it? How can you better live from that perfect love today?*

No Matter What...

There is no fear in love. And that's exactly what you have:
a perfect love from the God who created you. A God who
says, "Do not fear, for I love you just as you are, here,
today."

HOPE

PART TEN

A Thrill of Hope

The hope of good people ends in celebration.
Proverbs 10:28

A thrill of hope,
the weary world rejoices.
Adolphe Adams

THERE ARE FEW things more encouraging that hopeful words from a friend.

"The Whisper Test" is the story of a little girl who, like all of us at times, needed encouragement. Written by Mary Ann Bird, she tells her own story of being different, teased, and one day, encouraged:

> "I grew up knowing I was different, and I hated it. I was born with a cleft palate, and when I started school, my classmates made it clear to me how I must look to others; a little girl with a misshapen lip, crooked nose, lopsided teeth and garbled speech.
>
> "When schoolmates would ask, 'What happened to your lip?' I'd tell them I'd fallen and cut it on a piece

of glass. Somehow it seemed more acceptable to have suffered an accident than to have been born different. I was convinced that no one outside my family could love me. Then I entered Mrs. Leonard's second-grade class. Mrs. Leonard was round and pretty and fragrant, with shining brown hair and warm, dark, smiling eyes. Everyone adored her. But no one came to love her more than I did. And for a special reason.

"The time came for annual hearing tests given at our school. I could barely hear out of one ear and was not about to reveal something else that would single me out as different. So I cheated.

"The 'whisper test' required each child to go to the classroom door, turn sideways, close one ear with a finger, while the teacher whispered something from her desk, which the child repeated. Then the same for the other ear. Nobody checked how tightly the untested ear was covered, so I merely pretended to block mine. As usual, I was last. But all through the testing I wondered what Mrs. Leonard might say to me. I knew from previous years that the teacher whispered things like 'The sky is blue' or 'Do you have new shoes?'

"My time came. I turned my bad ear toward her, plugging up the other just enough to be able to hear. I waited, and then came the words that God has surely put into her mouth, seven words that changed my life forever.

"Mrs. Leonard, the teacher I adored, said softly, 'I

wish you were my little girl.'"[28]

Hopeful words can be thrilling. They can lift you from the depths, take you to a place you'd long forgotten.

You must never lose hope, never be afraid to hope.

Hope is the essential ingredient in you going for...anything. Before anyone else has to believe it, you have to believe it. You have to hope. Like Mrs. Leonard reminded Mary Ann, there's always reason to hope.

Hope when you're lost.
Hope when you're alone.
Hope when you've failed.
Hope when things get tough.
Hope when no one seems to care.
Hope when the future is uncertain.
Hope.

Where have you lost hope?
Where can you find more hope?
What are you hoping for today?

No Matter What...

Never lose hope. Keep reaching out. We need you today.

Stop Apologizing; We Need You

For God did not give us a spirit of timidity,
but of power, love, and self-discipline.
1 Timothy 1:7

Do the thing you fear most,
and the death of fear is certain.
Mark Twain

MAKE NO APOLOGIES for being the person God created you to be.

Last week, I called a friend of mine named Sara. She'd recently lost her sister to cancer, and I called to offer Sara prayer, encouragement, and peace. We talked for a while about how she was doing, what she needed, and I prayed for her. Right before we hung up, I asked,

"Is there anything else you need?"

"Well, Kevin," Sara said, changing the conversation, "yes there is. I know you called to encourage me, but I have a thought for you."

"Sure," I offered a hesitant response. "What is it?"

"Well, the past two months have been tough. I've been committed to my sister, busy at work, and I haven't been able to go to church this whole time. So, I've been listening to a lot of podcasts, in particular, your podcast. And not just the recent episodes, I've been listening to the back catalog of sermons you've given over the years. They're great. Thank you for making them available. There is something I've noticed though."

"Oh yeah, what is it?"

"Yes. You apologize. A lot. Especially right before you have something challenging for us to hear. You say things like, 'Forgive me, but…' and 'I'm sorry, I hope this doesn't offend you too much, but…'

"Kevin, stop apologizing. I don't know if you're afraid of what you have to say, if you care too much what people think about you, or you just don't want to ruffle any feathers. But, you need to stop apologizing. When you've got something to say, say it. We're listening. We trust you. Lead us."

Standing in my office holding my phone, I was blown away at the courageous encouragement Sara was offering me.

"I know you called to encourage me," she went on, "and I appreciate it. But, Kevin, stop apologizing. We need you."

When the call was over, I stood in silence, reflecting on the conversation I'd just had. A few minutes later, I grabbed the nearest dry erase marker and wrote "Stop Apologizing" as big as I could atop the whiteboard beside my desk. Wow. Was Sara right? Was I afraid of what people thought? Was I holding back? Why didn't I believe in what it was I wanted to say?

What about you? What are you apologizing for?
Are you holding back in any way?
Are you timid? Why? Why are you apologizing?

Second Timothy 1:7 is often used in athletics circles, and for good reason. It says, "God doesn't give us a spirit of timidity, but of power, love, and self-discipline." If you're timid, that's not God in you. It's something else, from somewhere else.

Stop apologizing.

No Matter What...

God doesn't want you apologizing for the gifts and talents He's given you. Own them. Use them. Help as many people with them as you can.

You Won't Regret This

Be strong and do not give up,
for your work will be rewarded.
2 Chronicles 15:7

There's two kinds of pain in sports;
the pain of discipline and the pain of regret.
Jeff Blatnick

"I REALLY REGRET that workout," said no one ever.

It's okay to regret eating the whole tub of ice cream. It's probably a good idea to regret that weekend in Vegas. Everybody regrets not studying for the final exam that was worth half the grade. But, you'll never regret reaching out for the person God created you to be.

Whatever it is God's put in your heart to do, you won't regret going for it.

You won't regret giving today your all.
You won't regret doing things the right way.
You won't regret encouraging your teammates when they're down.
You won't regret staying after practice and putting in extra reps.

You won't regret getting enough sleep tonight.
You won't regret eating well, hustling, staying positive, and finishing what you started.

Second Chronicles 5 says, "God rewards those who don't give up." It's how the universe works. Those who work hard, persevere, and adjust when the course calls for it are the ones who find the reward God wants for them.

I've never met a college student who, at the end of his or her athletic career, regretted giving it a go at being a student-athlete. Whether they were among the few who had a career in athletics after college or, like most, they moved on to a new thing, not one regretted giving their dream a shot, regardless of how long it lasted or didn't last.

Are you ready to give up?
Are you getting tired?
What will you regret more: not trying, or going for it and receiving whatever reward God's got in store?

See yourself 10 years from now. You won't regret having given today your all.

No Matter What...

No one regrets giving his or her dreams a shot. You won't regret this either.

It's Never Too Late

It's not too late to come back to God...
Here's why: God is kind and merciful.
Joel 2:14-15

Being realistic is the most commonly
traveled path to mediocrity.
Will Smith

IT'S NEVER TOO late.

After his retirement in 1972, at the ripe old age of 71, Norman Maclean could have stepped away from his professional life with dignity. Decades of service as a professor of English literature at the University of Chicago, his career spoke for itself. There was nothing more for Maclean to prove, no one asking him for anything. He could rest and finally enjoy his retirement. But he didn't.

One person felt that Norman wasn't quite done, not yet. One person did want more from Maclean. That person was Norman Maclean himself.

Norman Maclean always wanted to try his hand at writing a

book, and he thought he had a good story, too. So at 71, even though some suggested it might not be worth the effort, Maclean retreated to a cabin in his childhood home of Montana. He emerged nearly two years later offering the world *A River Runs Through It*, the true story of Maclean's childhood growing up in Montana. The book is now one of America's greatest literary treasures. It went on to be nominated for the Pulitzer Prize in 1977 and propelled Norman Maclean to national prominence.[29]

At 73, when most of us are satisfied to hang it up and live out our days in peace and quiet, Norman Maclean became a great American writer.

It's never too late to be who you might have been.

I've met many athletes over the years who believed they missed their chance. They think they blew it. They didn't win a starting job or they didn't have a good game or they ended up just a few seconds short of the qualifying time, so they thought it was over. But what was over? What did they lose? Sure, perhaps they've since retired from their sport. Maybe they didn't make it to the Olympics, but all's not lost.

Remember, God is more concerned with who we're becoming than where it is we end up. Losing is an event, not a character trait. So your project failed. You didn't make it. But maybe you did. Maybe the project failing and you having to retire are exactly what God wanted for you in the first place. Maybe you'd never realize who God invites you to become if you hadn't first gone for it and fallen short.

Who you might have been has less to do with what you could've accomplished and more to do with your character. Sure, it may be too late to win those games and achieve those medals, but it's never too late to become the person God longed for you to be in the first place.

Who did you want to become?
Is it too late? Why?
How might God still be working?
How might this new chapter be exactly what you need to be more whole, more grateful, more alive and clear?

No Matter What...

It's never too late to reap the blessings of having gone for it. Keep trusting God today. Keep reaching out.

God's Not Done

Don't panic. I'm with you.
There's no need to fear for I'm your God.
I'll give you strength. I'll help you.
I'll hold you steady, keep a firm grip on you.
Isaiah 41:10

We are unfinished creatures — longing,
reaching, stretching towards fulfillment.
Eugene Peterson

IF GOD'S NOT done with you yet, why would you give up?

Maewyn Succat was born in 373 AD near modern-day Dumbarton, Scotland. At the age of 16, raiders kidnapped young Succat and took him to Ireland where he was sold to the Irish chieftain Miliucc. For six years, he lived as a slave and knew nothing of his home, his family, or what his life would become. For now, he was a shepherd-slave, often tending sheep in the hills alone for months on end. He never lost his faith in God, though. He would later write,

"The love and fear of God more and more inflamed my heart; my faith enlarged, my spirit augmented, so that I said a hundred prayers by day and almost as many by night. I arose before day in the snow, in the frost, and the rain, yet I received no harm, nor was I affected with slothfulness. For then the spirit of God was warm within me."

Then, one day in a dream, Succat heard a voice calling out to him, "Thy ship is ready for thee." Succat fled his master's home that very night. He traveled nearly 200 miles by foot toward the sea and caught a ship home to Britain. He found his way back to his family, and he gave his life to the church. He became a priest and, eventually, a bishop. He could have lived out his days in peace and quiet, but in 432 AD, he heard another voice.

"And there I saw a vision during the night, a man coming from the west; his name was Victorious, and had with him many letters; he gave me one to read, and in the beginning of it was a voice from Ireland, 'Come to us, O holy youth, and walk among us.' With this I was feelingly touched, and could read no longer. I then awoke."

Maewyn Succat, better known to us today as St. Patrick, returned to Ireland later that year. The once shepherd-slave, now Catholic bishop, returned to the land of his captors and experienced the blessing of God unlike any missionary before him. Maewyn Succat's ministry in Ireland founded over 300 churches, baptized more than 120,000 people, and St. Patrick became known as the man who "found Ireland all heathen and left it all Christian."

God's not done with you yet. Your season may be over, your career in the distant past, but God is always moving. And God ever wants you to trust Him. Today, God invites you to go for it, to go for something, to join Him in His work of renewal in and through your life.

Where have you given up on God?
How have you moved on?
What might God still be doing in your life? Through your life?

No Matter What...

God is not done with you or him or her or anybody yet.
Open your eyes, and see what God is doing.

God Loves You Too Much

I am doing a new thing!
Now it springs up; do you not perceive it?
I am making a way in the wilderness
and streams in the wasteland.
Isaiah 43:18-19

God loves you just the way you are,
but He refuses to leave you that way.
Max Lucado

GOD LOVES YOU too much.

Over the years I've had hundreds, if not thousands, of conversations with student-athletes and coaches. Identity, purpose, mindset, excuses, others, commitment, adversity, boundaries, fear, and hope: these ten themes represent the most prevalent talking points from all of those discussions.

And if I take a big step back, though, maybe we only ever talked about one thing: transformation.

A main premise to this book, and to my greater work as a chaplain and pastor, is that God's love is vast and beyond measure.

God loves you, and God loves me. We don't have to do or prove anything to be recipients of that love. It's the truest thing about us. God loves you just as you are, today. Here. You don't need to go for anything. You have nothing to prove. You can rest in this love.

I've also encouraged you, though, to go for it. Know that God loves you just as you are, but that God also gave you gifts, talent, and opportunities so that you'd reach out for Him, so that you'd trust Him and create something good in the world with everything He's given you.

And what is God doing?

Isaiah 43:18-19 says, "I am doing a new thing! I am making a way in the wilderness and streams in the wasteland." God's doing a new thing. God is taking broken things and making them whole again. God is taking people in despair and offering them hope. He is bringing light to dark places and giving a voice to the voiceless. This is what God does.

And so, yeah, God loves you just as you are, but God loves you too much to leave you that way.

God wants to give you a secure identity.
God wants to transform your mind and give you a regenerative thought life.
God wants you to stop making excuses and start taking responsibility for your gifts and talents.
God wants you to see the people around you and join Him in serving them.
God wants you to be faithful to the commitments you've made.
God wants you to overcome adversity and grow from it.
God wants you to take care of yourself and steward your time

and energy well.

God wants you to not be afraid anymore.
God wants you to keep believing, to keep reaching out, no matter what.

> *What needs to be made new in your life?*
> *Where is God inviting you to join Him in making others' lives new as well?*

No Matter What...

God loves you too much to leave you where you are today.
He invites you to join Him in making all things new.

God Is For You

For in God, we live and
move and have our being.
Acts 17:28

How many things have to happen to you
before something occurs to you?
Robert Frost

GOD IS FOR us. We must never forget this.

Today, on our annual trip around the sun, we'll travel 1.603 million miles at a speed of 19 miles per second, or 67,000 miles per hour. During this journey, we'll spin around Earth's axis at a rate of 1,040 mph. This daily rotation is necessary to our survival because it gives us days and nights, seasons, appropriate atmospheric pressure, and tides. To keep us alive on our trip, we're going to need oxygen. It's a good thing, then, that a single, 100-foot tree with a base diameter of 18 inches produces 6,000 pounds of oxygen every day, or 260 pounds of oxygen a year. Two adult trees of this size can adequately provide enough oxygen for a family of four. We're also going to need power. Great news, the sun delivers more solar energy to Earth in an hour than the entire world's population consumes in one year.

Without lifting a finger, Earth will stay in orbit, its rotation will maintain a constant speed, you'll have adequate temperatures, seasons, and atmospheric pressure, not to mention enough oxygen and water to live. All that, and the sun will distribute enough sunlight for photosynthetic life to thrive and for you and me to power our homes, classrooms, and the places we work.

If you're like me, you've probably never taken the time to appreciate any of this. Your prayers rarely include thanks for the sun, the trees, Earth's rotation or the fact that we stay in orbit. I don't say thank-you for any of these things, not because I don't need them. I do; we all do. No, I don't give thanks because I'm not paying attention.

There's a phenomenon in psychology called perceptual blindness, also known as inattentional blindness. It describes our inability to recognize an unexpected stimulus that is in plain sight. For a vast number of reasons, we fail to see all that is happening in and around our lives. But just because we're not paying attention doesn't mean some things aren't essential to our existence and present all the time.

Acts 17 says, "God gives all people life and breath and everything else. In Him, we live and move and have our being." Job 33:4 says, "The Spirit of God made me what I am, and the breath of God gives me life!" Romans 8 says, "If God is for us, who can be against us?"

Is it possible that God is so good at doing what God does that we're blind to everything God is doing? Keeping us in orbit, giving us life, breath, oxygen and power, God is busy holding everything together. What will it take for us to notice?

Never forget this: God is for you. God is for us all. He gives and sustains life for you, me, your friends and enemies alike. If you're struggling, timid, frustrated, discouraged, or worse, remember that God isn't far away. He hasn't left you stranded, alone or out to dry. God is doing so much for you all the time.

What is God constantly doing for you that you've not been paying attention to?
How is God providing for you today?
Where is God working even now for your benefit?

G.K. Chesterton said, "How much happier you would be, how much more of you there would be, if the hammer of a higher God could smash your small cosmos." May you have courage to see what you've been missing.

No Matter What...

God is for you. God is doing so much that you just
can't see.

Guidance Is a Rope

Let the wise listen and add to their learning,
and let the discerning get guidance.
Proverbs 1:5

Change awaits us.
What is decisive is our deciding.
Gregory Boyle

GOD'S WILL IS not a map. God's will is a way.

More than half the discussions I've had with athletes and coaches over the years are about one thing: what should I do next?

How should I move forward?
What does God want me to do?
Where does God want me to go?
Who does God want me to marry?

Should I retire from my sport or should I keep playing?
Is this the right degree path or should I select a different major?
What should I do after athletics?
What's God's will for my life?

When an athlete or coach asks my opinion with any of these questions, there is always another underlying question, maybe even an assumption, and it goes something like this: "God surely has a plan for my life, doesn't He?"

My response is always the same: "Yes, God surely has a plan for your life. God wants you to make a decision. God's plan is for you to decide."

Everyone needs guidance. We all want direction. Sometimes, there is a right choice and a wrong choice. But, more often than not, there is a right choice and a right choice. More often than not, all the options are fine options. God will be with us whatever we decide. God is just waiting for us to make a choice.

Tim Keller says, "God's guidance isn't something God gives; it's something God does.

In Hebrew, the word for guidance is *tachbulah*, which literally means "rope." That may seem strange, but when much of the Old Testament was written, the primary means of long-distance travel was by ship. Ropes held these vessels together. Ropes were used for rigging, casting, anchoring, towing, and steering the rudder. On a sailboat, knowing how the ropes work is everything. This is where the saying "show 'em the ropes" comes from.

Now, the purpose of ropes on a sailboat wasn't to tell the ship which way to go. That was up to the captain. The purpose of the ropes was to hold the ship together. God's guidance works the same way.

God's will for your life is to hold you together. God's purpose isn't to tell you what decisions to make, but to show you how to make healthy decisions.

What decisions are you struggling to make?
What would it take for you to just make a decision and trust that God is going to hold you together no matter the outcome?

No Matter What...

Do you want to know what God's will is for your life? Make a choice.

Gratitude Is the Way

A cheerful heart fills the day with song.
Proverbs 15:15

To be grateful is to recognize the
love of God in everything.
Thomas Merton

YOU HAVE SO much to be thankful for.

Life	*Health*	*A vision*
Friends	*Support*	*A dream*
Family	*Coaches*	*A goal*
Talent	*Trainers*	*Today*
Intelligence	*Professors*	
Opportunity	*Teammates*	

Taking just 5 minutes and reflecting upon any of these could change your day today.

Jesus said in Matthew 6, "The eye is the lamp of the body. If your eyes are healthy, your whole body will be full of light. But if your eyes are unhealthy, your whole body will be full of darkness. If then the light within you is darkness, how great is that darkness!"

Gratitude is God's way of turning the lights on. When we begin to see and be grateful for God's provision in our lives, our well-being increases.

There are hundreds of books, scores of articles, and a handful of scientific studies that prove just that. The benefits of being grateful include a strengthening of your emotions and an increase in your faith, and it makes you a healthier person. One such study suggests that a five-minute-per-day gratitude journal gives you 10 percent less chronic pain, 16 percent fewer physical ailments, increases your chances of exercise by 19 percent, gives you 5 percent more sleep, and promotes 25 percent better sleep. Gratitude significantly decreases your systolic blood pressure, and it leaves you feeling emotionally capable: less envious, less self-centered, less materialistic, more content, spiritually-centered, more optimistic, friendlier, and with greater overall self-esteem.[30]

What do you have to be thankful for today?
Who do you have to be thankful for today?
Where has God provided?
How is God meeting your needs?

If you're going to go for it, be grateful. As Jesus suggested, let your eyes be full of light. In all of the ups and downs of putting yourself out there, you're going to need to see clearly.

No Matter What...

Be grateful. It can change your life.

No Matter What

See what kind of love the Father
has given to us, that we should be called
children of God; and so we are.
1 John 3:1

No matter what: we'll love you.
Hoke Knox

AT SOME POINT in life, everyone asks himself or herself this question: "What am I supposed to do with my life? Now, why I, only an elementary-school-aged-kid at the time, would be so worked up over something so far off, I don't know. But for me that night, it was real. And what I didn't know, I decided my dad had the answer.

I ran downstairs, jumped up in his chair, and pushed his newspaper aside. "Dad," I asked, "What do you and mom want me to be when I grow up?"

"What do you mean?" his face looked puzzled holding back a smile.

"I'm trying to figure out what I'm supposed to do with my life," I explained. "Whatever you guys want me to do, I'll do that. Just tell me."

The confidence in his response gave me the impression he and mom had already talked about it. "Kevin, you can do whatever you want to when the time comes."

I sat still for a moment, looked over at the fire in the fireplace, and thought about his words. "Okay." I jumped down and ran upstairs as dad returned to his reading. It didn't take five minutes for me to realize I didn't like his answer. Running back downstairs, stopping this time at the foot of his chair, I asked again.

"Dad, I'm serious," I said. "What do you guys want me to be? Just tell me, and I'll do that."
He responded with the same answer: "Kevin, I can't tell you what you're supposed to do when you're older. Whatever you choose, your mother and I will be happy. We'll support you."

"Really? You don't have anything you want me to do, not even a suggestion?"

"Whatever you enjoy doing or find you're good at when the time comes, we'll support you. You get to choose."

"Okay," I said a second time before retreating back upstairs.

Again, not five minutes later, I ran downstairs a third time. "Dad, the thing is, I don't know what

I'm supposed to do. I really don't know. Please, just tell me."

"Kevin," Dad scooted to the edge of his chair and leaned in as he spoke, "the only thing your mother and I want for you is this: to know that God loves you and we love you. No matter what you do, no matter where you go, we'll love you."

"So whatever I choose, you'll be okay with that?" I asked.

"Yes. No matter what, we'll love you."

And for the third and final time, I said again, only this time I meant it, "Okay."

To this day, my dad's words tower over me:

"No matter what. We'll love you."

Somebody once told me we only make a few decisions in life—who to marry, where to live, what to do for a living, and a handful of other big decisions. All the other choices we make along the way are simply a byproduct of those few, big decisions. If that's true, then conversations are like decisions; some are bigger than others. Like a song on repeat, certain conversations play in the background of everything we think and do. This conversation is like that. It's been on repeat for years. Fortunately for me, it's a good song, and it's played the loudest when I've needed it the most.

No matter what, God loves you, too.

Like my dad said to me, God says to you, "No matter what, I'll love you. May this be your song. In it, may you find strength and courage and wisdom and hope for the rest of your life.

God loves you, no matter what.

Win or lose.
Succeed or fail.
Get there or fall short.
God's love for you will never change.

Do you believe this?
Do you understand the depth of God's love for you?
Do you believe a "no matter what" kind of love is even possible?
What will it take for you to receive it?
How can you trust it today?

The "no matter what"-ness of God's love is vast and beyond measure.

And that includes you too.

No Matter What...

God loves you. You don't have to go for anything. But because God loves you, you should.

Notes

1. McCormack, Mark H. *What They Don't Teach You at Harvard Business School.* Toronto: Bantam Books, 1986.

2. Ware, Bronnie. *The Top Five Regrets of the Dying: A Life Transformed by the Dearly Departing.* Australia: Hay House, 2012.

3. Hill, James J. *Touchstones of Success: A Book of Inspiration for Young Men.* Philadelphia, PA: The Vir Publishing Company, 1920.

4. Eby, EJ. "The Hidden Meaning of Just Do It." Dirt Simple (Blog). July, 2006. http://dirtsimple.org/2006/07/hidden-meaning-of-just-do-it.html.

5. Posnanski, Joe. "Simply Successful." Sports on Earth (Blog). October, 2012. http://www.sportsonearth.com/article/40063294/how-did-kansas-state-football-coach-bill-snyder-manage-to-put-his-team-in-national-title-conversation-again.

6. Dillard, Annie. *The Writing Life.* New York: Harper Perennial, 2013.

7. Goff, Bob. *Love Does: Discover a Secretly Incredible Life in an Ordinary World.* Nashville, TN.: Thomas Nelson, 2012.

8. Chandler, Steve. *Reinventing Yourself.* New Jersey: Career Press, 2005.

9. Achor, Shawn. *The Happiness Advantage: The Seven Principles of Positive Psychology That Fuel Success and Performance at Work.* First edition. Broadway Books, 2010.

10. Russert, Tim. *Big Russ and Me.* New York: Miramax, 2005.

11. Wooden, John, and Don Yaeger. *A Game Plan for Life: The Power of Mentoring.* New York: Bloomsbury USA, 2009.

12. Draegar, Lars. *Navy SEAL Training Guide: Mental Toughness.* Special Operations Media, 2013.

13. 2 Corinthians 10:5.

14. Palmer, Lisa. "What Are Extreme Runners Thinking?" Slate (Online Magazine). May, 2013. http://www.slate.com/articles/health_and_science/superman/2013/05/ultramarathon_runner_scott_jurek_extreme_athletes_determination_pain_and.html.

15. Philippians 4:12-13, NLT.

16. Spiegel, Alex. "What Heroin Addiction Tells Us About Changing Bad Habits." Morning Edition (Blog). January 2015. http://www.npr.org/sections/health-shots/2015/01/05/371894919/what-heroin-addiction-tells-us-about-changing-bad-habits.

17. Rohr, Richard. *Breathing Under Water: Spirituality And The Twelve Steps.* Ohio: Franciscan Media, 2011.

18. Elliot, Elisabeth. *Discipline: The Glad Surrender.* Michigan: Revell, 2006.

19. Miller, Donald. "Why People Are Drawn to Simplicity Over Truth." Storyline (Blog). August, 2014, http://storyline-blog.com/2016/07/11/why-people-are-drawn-to-simplicity-over-truth/.

20. Boyle, Greg. *Tattoos on the Heart: The Power of Boundless Compassion.* New York, NY: Free Press, 2010.

21. The West Wing. "Noel." #32. Directed by Thomas Schlamme. Written by Aaron Sorkin. NBC, December, 2000.

22. "Procrastination: Readers tales of epic time-wasting." BBC (Online Magazine) August, 2013. http://www.bbc.com/news/magazine-19396204.

23. Putnam RD. *Bowling Alone: The Collapse and Revival of American Community.* New York: Simon & Schuster; 2000.

24. Colvin, Geoff. *Talent Is Overrated: What Really Separates World-Class Performers from Everybody Else.* New York: Portfolio, 2008.

25. Dweck, Carol S. Mindset: The New Psychology of Success. New York: Random House, 2006.

26. Gladwell, Malcolm. *David and Goliath: Underdogs, Misfits, and the Art of Battling Giants.* First edition. New York: Little, Brown and Company, 2013.

27. Walker, Karen Thompson. "What Fear Can Teach Us", TEDTALK (Video file), June, 2012, https://www.ted.

com/talks/karen_thompson_walker_what_fear_can_teach_us?language=en.

28. Fields, J. Brene Brown on the power of being vulnerable [Video file]. Retrieved from http://www.youtube.com/watch?v=Sd3DYvB-GyFs, 2012.

29. Frankl, Viktor E. Man's Search for Meaning: An Introduction to Logotherapy. New York: Simon & Schuster, 1984.

30. Foth, Dick. "The Heart Of The Matter: Words." Sermon, National Community Church, Washington, D.C., October 5, 2014.

31. Maclean, Norman. *A River Runs Through It, and Other Stories.* Chicago: University of Chicago Press, 1976.

32. Sansone, Randy A., and Lori A. Sansone. "Gratitude and Well Being: The Benefits of Appreciation." Psychiatry (Edgmont) 7.11 (2010): 18–22. Print.